MONISHA BHARADWAJ
INDIAN IN 6

MONISHA BHARADWAJ

Indian in 6

100 IRRESISTIBLE RECIPES THAT USE 6 INGREDIENTS OR LESS

KYLE BOOKS

As always – for Arrush and India Saayli

First published in Great Britain in 2005 by
Kyle Books
23 Howland Street
London W1T 4AY
general.enquiries@kylebooks.com
www.kylebooks.com

This edition first published in 2011

ISBN 978 0 85783 016 6

Senior Editor Stephanie Horner
Designer Geoff Hayes
Photographer Gus Filgate
Home Economist David Morgan
Production Sha Huxtable and Alice Holloway

A Cataloguing In Publication record for this title is available from the British Library.

Colour reproduction by Sang Choy
Printed and bound in China by Toppan Leefung Printing Ltd

Contents

Introduction

Most people, including those who love Indian food and cook it often, tend to think that it is a complicated cuisine, takes forever to make and needs a long list of ingredients to ensure the dish is delicious. My last book, *Stylish Indian in Minutes*, was about how good Indian recipes could be made very quickly with no loss in nutrition or taste; this one focuses on how to make it with just a few, good-quality ingredients.

Indian in 6 is certainly not about whittling down the number of ingredients in an authentic recipe just for the sake of a fancy cookbook. There is no doubt that many traditional Indian recipes do call for a vast number of ingredients and that they simply cannot be made without the entire list. However, equally, there are countless delectable dishes that use far fewer ingredients which are cooked daily in many Indian homes. Also, newer and better commercially available products (such as garam masala powder or faster cooking cuts of meat) mean that we need fewer ingredients to cook with. Many Indian homemakers today do not grind their own spices for garam masala or put tenderisers such as raw papaya into their marinades for meat as their grandmothers probably did.

Historically, home cooking in India has always been simple and unfussy. Women spent time making up their own spice powders such as garam masala or sambhar, their chutneys, relishes and jams, or storable snacks such as savouries or poppadums that could be served with a meal. This meant that many components of a meal were prepared in advance and the time spent each day in the kitchen was reduced. There would be fresh rice and rotis and a couple of vegetable dishes, even maybe a meat dish, but all this would be supplemented by prepared accompaniments to make the meal more varied.

Today we buy ready-made poppadums and preserves and our meals are less elaborate. Many young Indians are happy to eat roti or rice with a curry or a stir fry and a fresh salad. More emphasis is given to freshness and quality of ingredients. Also, large families living together are now a thing of the past and even in India most families are nuclear with both the husband and the wife in full-time work. All this requires a new way of managing the kitchen and even a very traditional housewife will quite happily buy ready-made rotis or canned cooked chickpeas. This was not always so. Cooks of previous generations would have us believe that unless everything was prepared freshly at home, just before serving, it could be no good!

Frankly, I too have reached the point where long lists of ingredients scare me. Although I learned hands-on the best of Indian cooking (both ingredient-heavy recipes as well as light, refreshing ones) in my family kitchen back in Bombay, I have found that as time goes by I spend my time experimenting with great new flavours and ingredients that simplify my cooking and give me the opportunity to create unusual combinations or to make healthier foods for my young family. The kids too love to join in the process and we come up with some wonderfully clean-tasting and uniquely spiced dishes! Kids have a knack of getting down to basics and we try to add just enough flavouring and spice to let the main ingredients shine right through.

Staple ingredients

Speaking of ingredients, here is a list of what I absolutely must keep a stock of in my store cupboard:

✝ **cans of beans**: chickpeas, red kidney beans, butter beans

✝ **cans of fruit**: pineapple, mango, mango purée, lychee

✝ **cans of peeled plum tomatoes**

✝ **cans of coconut milk, evaporated milk**

✝ **many kinds of nuts**: almonds, pistachios, cashews and peanuts

✝ **jars of mint sauce** (for instant mint chutney when you stir a bit into natural yogurt!)

✝ **tamarind pulp, desiccated coconut**

✝ **brown cane sugar**

✝ **spices and spice mixtures**: black mustard seeds (Indian cooks do not use the yellow ones except for pickling vegetables and fruit), cardamom (buy whole green pods and crush the seeds whenever a recipe calls for powdered cardamom seeds), chilli powder, cloves, coriander seed powder, cumin seeds, garam masala, peppercorns, tandoori masala powder (a red spice mixture to rub onto foods to be barbecued or cooked in the tandoori style; check, though, for additives such as colourants), turmeric powder, saffron strands

✝ **curry leaves** (these are bought fresh and can be dried at home; the dried ones last for up to a month). They are available in Indian grocery shops and have a powerful curry-like flavour. Used mostly in south Indian cookery.

✝ **various lentils, flours** (atta is wholewheat flour and is used for rotis and parathas. It cannot be substituted with plain flour. Gram flour is made from chickpeas) **and rice.**

I always use basmati rice. Good rice is like wine, it improves with age. Very good-quality basmati can be left to age and mature for up to 10 years. Old rice cooks better and remains fluffy whereas new rice becomes sticky when cooked. There is no way of determining the age of the rice in western supermarkets but many grocers in India will tell you the age of the rice you are buying.

To cook rice, wash it in several changes of water until the water runs clear. This is to remove traces of starch or preserving powders. Then add twice the amount of cold water (so for 110g (4oz) rice add 225 ml (8fl oz) water). Bring to the boil, stir and lower the heat. Simmer with a lid on for about 10–12 minutes until done. Do not open the pan for a further 10 minutes as the rice fluffs up in the steam. Always use a heavy-bottomed pan as the rice might get scorched at the bottom in a light one.

Other ingredients

✝ **Coriander leaves** In Indian shops fresh coriander is sold bunched, attached to its roots. If you buy it like this, wash the leaves and stems to remove any grit and dry before chopping. The leaves are much used as a flavouring in savoury dishes and as a garnish, either chopped or sprigged.

✝ **Cumin seeds** Many recipes call for roasted cumin seed powder. To make this, simply dry roast a teaspoonful of cumin seeds in a frying pan. As the seeds begin to darken, shake them a little to prevent them burning then tip into a mortar. Bash with your pestle to turn them to a powder.

✝ **Flaked rice** In India flaked rice is sold as 'pawa' or 'poha'. This is found in all Indian shops in the West. The flaked rice you get in supermarkets is harder in texture and needs to be soaked for much longer than pawa.

✝ **Ginger and garlic** To make the ginger-garlic paste used throughout this book, use equal quantities of each, peel and whizz in a blender until fairly smooth. I usually make this paste in big batches and freeze it in thin sheets between plastic. Of course, you will have to put the frozen sheets of ginger and garlic in big freezer containers otherwise everything will smell, from your ice cream to ice cubes! Just break off bits when you need them and add straight to the pan.

✝ **Mango** Ask any Indian what the best mangoes are and you will hear 'Alphonso'. These mangoes come from the state of Maharashtra. They are sweet, juicy and smooth with very few fibres and a scent like saffron.

To prepare a mango, slice off the top and cut the cheeks away from the central stone. Then gently cut the flesh within the cheeks in a crisscross

fashion to make small squares. Run a knife under the squares to loosen them from the skin. Peel off the skin from any flesh attached to the central stone and dice this flesh too. The reward for the cook is that you get to sit in a corner and suck on the stone for as long as like!

✝ **Sugar** Some Indian recipes use white sugar but others are enhanced with jaggery – dehydrated sugarcane juice. It has a musky caramel-like flavour and a texture that is sticky yet crumbly, and it melts very easily. It can be bought in Indian shops but if you cannot find jaggery, substitute soft brown sugar – although the taste will vary.

✝ **Silver leaf or varq** This is available in most Indian shops. It is sold as fine sheets between greaseproof papers and is quite sticky. To use it, simply open up the paper and pat the silver leaf onto the food you want to decorate. Putting it into water sometimes makes it easier to use. It has no taste but looks wonderfully festive on meats, rice and sweets.

The challenge in writing this book was to produce a selection of delectable recipes that recognise that today's busy homemakers want to create fantastic Indian meals without the fuss of complicated or time-consuming recipes. I wanted to capture the flavours, colours and aromas that are the essence of Indian cuisine to create dishes that use no more than 6 ingredients, but remain authentic, modern and, above all, very simple. Apart from the 6 in each recipe, I was allowed 3 'free' staple ingredients. I chose:

✝ **Sunflower oil**
✝ **Salt**
✝ **Ginger-garlic paste** (because they are almost always used together)

Measures

Although all the recipes in this book have been measured and tested, I believe that the best cooks use a big dose of intuition and judgement. I have found over the many years I've spent teaching and demonstrating Indian cooking that, however accurate an ingredient list may be, different people use different ones or can only source particular ingredients. I recall on one occasion I had asked for basmati rice to make plain boiled rice and instead I was given a packet of easy-cook rice with the explanation that it would cut down on the cooking time. In fact it did not, and the end result was far from what I had hoped for.

To touch and smell your ingredients as well as taste them, both as they cook and when they are ready to serve. This sensory experience will provide you with the best possible clues about how the dish will turn out. A friend of mine can judge whether a dish needs more salt simply by smelling it!

Feel free to alter the amount of chilli powder I specify in the recipes according to your own preference for mildness or heat. I tend to be conservative in my use of chillies and chilli powder as I do not like my food overwhelmed by spice and heat.

Equipment

Most Indian cooks use a heavy kadhai or wok for stir frying and deep frying. An Indian wok is heavier than the Chinese one as it is used to cook food for longer periods of time.

Another important piece of equipment is the grinder which is essential for making curry pastes and chutneys. I use a large blender for big quantities and a small coffee mill for spice powders and smaller spice blends. A pestle and mortar set is also useful.

Much of Indian cooking is done in one pot, beginning with a tiny amount of oil to fry the spice seeds and then the sequence continues. Many cooks find that a pressure cooker absorbs these processes beautifully and it will drastically cut down on cooking time. I use my pressure cooker every day to cook meat, potatoes and lentils. I have not used a pressure cooker in these recipes, however, as it is not an item that is popular with western cooks. Having said that, good quality, heavy-bottomed pans are very suitable.

Preparing great Indian meals doesn't have to be a hard slog, so here's to many fun days in the kitchen. Enjoy!

Indians swear by their breakfast and each region of the country has a spectacular variety of hot and cold dishes to start the day. From the south come steaming hot rice cakes called idlis and pancakes known as dosas. Traditionally these are served on a banana leaf, accompanied by an assortment of colourful chutneys, such as a green-tinted coconut and raw mango one or a fiery-red one made with dried chilli and mustard seeds.

In the area around Mumbai, spiced rice flakes called pawa, cooked with onions, potatoes or green peas are most popular. Further north, in Gujarat, sweet, syrupy fritters called jalebis are served with the contrasting taste of crunchy, savoury wafers or gathia.

In north India, where farming is the main occupation of the villagers, flavours are much more robust and breakfasts are quite hearty. Here many versions of potato bread or parathas are washed down with cooling glassfuls of lassi.

Elsewhere in the country, fried bread is served with spiced potatoes in the classic combination of 'puri-bhaji'. Often, sprouted lentils are combined with fresh homemade yogurt and eaten with toasted bread. Porridge made from cracked wheat or oats is served, either sweetened with sugar or accompanied by hot spicy pickles made with lemon or raw mango.

And, of course, fresh fruit – such as mango, watermelon, papaya, bananas, sapota (known as chikoo in India), pomegranate and apples – is always served as an excellent way to begin the day.

Breakfasts

PORRIDGE OATS WITH CARDAMOM AND SAFFRON

Elaichi Dalia

Various kinds of breakfast porridges are popular all over India, some sweet, others savoury. The most delicious ones are made with cracked wheat or oats and give a glorious burst of early morning energy that lasts right up to lunchtime. I sometimes serve this with salt instead of sugar for those not blessed with a sweet tooth. Serves 4

Preparation time: 2 minutes **Cooking time:** 10 minutes or less

2 green cardamom pods
300g (10oz) instant porridge oats
Few strands of saffron
Milk to taste
Sugar to taste

1 Remove the cardamom seeds from the pods and discard the skins. (I sometimes put these discarded skins into my sugar jar for a bit of fragrance). Crush the seeds in a mortar.

2 Put the oats into a heavy-bottomed saucepan and cover with water. Bring to the boil on a high heat then reduce to a simmer, adding more water as necessary to keep the porridge nice and moist.

3 Add the saffron and remove the pan from the heat when the oats are cooked.

4 Sprinkle in the crushed cardamom and serve hot with milk and sugar.

YOGURT SMOOTHIE WITH TROPICAL FRUIT AND NUTS

Mewa Lassi

Great jugs of lassi, or whisked yogurt, are enjoyed as a traditional breakfast in the villages of north India. It is usually salted, served with chunky potato bread called parathas. This city version is a bit more stylish and power-breakfast oriented. The fruit and nut kick-start the day beautifully and the yogurt keeps the digestion happy. Serves 4

Preparation time: 10 minutes

150g (5oz) any tropical fruit, such as mango, guava or pineapple, peeled and prepared weight
2 tablespoons mixed nuts
300g (10oz) natural bio yogurt
Sugar to taste

1 Put everything in a blender and whizz until smooth. If you cannot get all the nut pieces to grind down, just leave them in and enjoy the crunch in the finished drink.

2 Dilute with a little water and serve immediately.

Gode Pohe

favourite childhood breakfast of mine, which I still love making when I
ancy something sweet and nourishing after a tiring working week. Indian
ce flakes are readily available and are used in both sweet and savoury
ishes. Choose the 'medium thick' variety for this dish rather than 'fine'
awa. Serves 4

Preparation time: 5 minutes + 5 minutes soaking
Cooking time: 5 minutes

00g (10oz) Indian rice flakes (pawa)
rown sugar to taste
eeds from 2 green cardamom pods, crushed
tablespoons freshly grated or desiccated coconut

1 Soak the rice flakes in water for 5 minutes and drain.

2 Mix all the ingredients together and heat very gently in a heavy-
bottomed pan until the sugar just begins to melt. Serve warm.

RICE STRANDS WITH MUSTARD SEED AND CASHEW NUTS

Seviyan Usli

A fragrant dish that comes from south India, this breakfast is both filling as well as delicious. I have eaten the best usli in a thousand-year-old, gorgeously carved temple near Goa, where hundreds of devotees are offered fresh, hot meals through the day. Serves 4

Preparation time: 10 minutes + 10 minutes soaking
Cooking time: 10 minutes

2 tablespoons sunflower oil
1/2 teaspoon black mustard seeds
5 fresh curry leaves
2 dried red chillies, stalks pinched off, seeds shaken out
10 whole cashew nuts, soaked in water for 10 minutes
300g (10oz) rice noodles, broken into 2.5cm (1in) bits and soaked in water for 10 minutes
1 teaspoon sugar
Salt

1 Heat the oil in a shallow wok and add the mustard seeds. Wait until they start to pop and add the curry leaves and the dried red chillies.

2 Drain the cashew nuts and add to the wok. Fry for 1 minute and stir in the drained rice noodles.

3 Sprinkle with sugar and salt. Cover the wok with a lid and cook the noodles for 5 minutes.

4 Serve hot.

HERBY ONION FLAVOURED EGG TOAST

Anda Pav

This is the Indian street version of French toast. Many workers often leav home early to travel great distances to their jobs but still find the time for a breakfast stop outside the railway station before catching the train. This is usually at one of the many little carts selling hot egg toasts with tomato ketchup. I often serve this breakfast on Sundays, and it is a great favourit with the kids. Serves 4

Preparation time: 10 minutes **Cooking time:** 10 minutes

1 onion, chopped
1 green chilli, chopped
1/2 teaspoon ginger-garlic paste
4 large eggs, beaten
2 tablespoons fresh coriander leaves, chopped
Salt
Sunflower oil for shallow frying
8 slices bread, white or brown

1 Put the onion, chilli, ginger-garlic paste, eggs, coriander leaves and sal in a large bowl and mix well.

2 Heat some oil in a large frying pan.

3 Dip the slices of bread into the egg mixture and shallow fry, 2 at a time on both sides, until they are golden and crispy at the edges.

4 Serve hot with ketchup. Any leftover egg can be scrambled and serve as a topping.

If you walk into an Indian home at dinnertime, chances are that there will be no starters or soups in sight. In a traditional meal all the courses are served at the same time and what we call starters are often accompaniments to the main meal.

However, with greater numbers of people entertaining these days for business or pleasure and with the sit-down 'thali' meal – where all the dishes, sweet and savoury, are served simultaneously in small metal bowls on a metal platter – being replaced by more informal gatherings and stand-up buffets, easy to serve soups or finger food starters have become a good way to get the meal going.

Starters are served in small quantities to whet the appetite and so they are quite piquantly flavoured and always beautifully presented. In fact, chefs in many large hotels in India compete with each other in creating surprising and sometimes dazzling starters.

The style of soups varies from region to region. In the south, spicy lentil soups reign whereas in the north, creamy ones are favoured. The nation's absolute favourite is a legacy of the Raj – cream of tomato soup. It is even served to passengers in all of India's national trains between 6 and 7 in the evening.

Soups
&
Starters

CREAMY SPINACH AND COCONUT SOUP

Palak ka Shorba

POPPADUMS STUFFED WITH SPICED PRAWNS

Thinge ke Papad

This is a variation of the traditional cream of spinach soup. The nutmeg gives it warmth and lifts the bland smoothness of the spinach. I often contrast its rich jewel-green colour with glossy black soup plates for a touch of drama. Serves 4

Preparation time: 10 minutes **Cooking time:** 25 minutes

400g (14oz) fresh spinach
1 teaspoon garlic paste, freshly made
300ml (10fl oz) coconut milk
Salt
Few turns of the peppermill
Few scrapes of nutmeg

1 Bring the spinach to the boil in a little water and cook until tender. Cool and whizz with the water in a liquidiser until smooth.

2 Stir in the garlic paste and add the coconut milk.

3 Season with salt and pepper and heat through without boiling the soup, or the coconut milk may curdle it.

4 Serve hot with freshly scraped nutmeg on top.

Poppadums are quite popular all over India and are made from a variety of flours including sago, gram (chickpea) and rice. These crispy appetisers come in all shapes, sizes and colours but outside of India, yellow poppadums are most common and are served in restaurants as starters with mango chutney. Serves 4

Preparation time: 10 minutes **Cooking time:** 10 minutes

Sunflower oil for deep frying
1 tablespoon ginger-garlic paste
1/2 teaspoon chilli powder
1/2 teaspoon turmeric powder
4 tablespoons peeled, cooked prawns, finely chopped
Salt
4 poppadums

1 Heat 1 tablespoon of the oil in a saucepan and fry the ginger-garlic paste

2 Add the spice powders, give the mixture a good stir and add the prawns and salt. Cook for a few minutes until the mixture is dry. Reserve.

3 Cut each poppadum into quarters with a pair of scissors. Spread prawn mixture over half of them then gently place another quarter on top to sandwich the filling.

4 Heat the oil in a deep pan until nearly smoking. Hold a filled poppadum with a pair of tongs and fry quickly for a few seconds. Drain on kitchen paper and keep warm. Continue similarly with the rest of the quarters. Serve immediately with mango chutney.

Ajwainwali Makki

Baby corn is a relative newcomer to the Indian kitchen but it has quickly caught the fancy of cooks all over the country. It appears in stir fries, curries and salads, often combined with another recent entrant– the mushroom. Ajowan is a relative of dill with seeds that resemble small cumin seeds. They have a sharp hot taste and are considered to be an excellent digestive. *Serves 4*

Preparation time: 15 minutes **Cooking time:** 15 minutes

1 teaspoon ginger-garlic paste
1 tablespoon lemon juice
Salt
300g (10oz) baby corn
2 tablespoons gram flour
Pinch of ajowan (ajwain)
1 egg
1/2 teaspoon chilli powder
Sunflower oil for deep frying

1 Combine the ginger-garlic paste, lemon juice and salt in a bowl and use to marinate the baby corn for 10 minutes.

2 Meanwhile, mix together the gram flour, ajowan, egg, chilli powder and enough water to make a thick batter.

3 Heat the oil in a deep pan or wok. Dip a few baby corn in the batter and fry until crisp. Continue to fry the rest of the baby corn in similar batches.

4 Serve immediately. They go well with mint sauce or raita.

Murg Motiya Shorba

A beautiful ivory-coloured soup that is both rich and flavourful. The chicken, nuts and coconut milk are all velvety in taste and are given a lift by the fresh coriander. Serve this soup with crusty bread and a dollop of butter. Serves 4

Preparation time: 10 minutes + 30 minutes soaking
Cooking time: 35 minutes

150g (5oz) chicken breast, diced
2 tablespoons ginger-garlic paste
2 tablespoons cashew nuts, soaked in water for 30 minutes
300ml (10fl oz) coconut milk
Salt
Few fresh coriander stalks, chopped

1 Put the diced chicken with 300ml (10fl oz) water in a heavy-bottomed saucepan and bring to the boil. Reduce the heat and simmer until the chicken is cooked.

2 Whizz the ginger-garlic paste and drained cashew nuts with some of the coconut milk in a small blender until smooth.

3 Put the paste into a pan and stir in the rest of the coconut milk. Strain the chicken stock into the pan. Season with salt and heat through gently.

4 Shred the cooked chicken and divide it among 4 soup bowls. Pour in the soup.

5 Serve hot, garnished with the coriander.

Murg Chaat Kalia

This is one of the many chicken delicacies of north India. The 'black' spices are roasted to bring out their flavour and the red onion adds crunch as well as kick. I sometimes serve this salad or chaat as a light lunch with an accompaniment of fried potato wedges and fresh tomato slices. Serves 4

Preparation time: 10 minutes **Cooking time:** 25 minutes

10 cloves
1 teaspoon cardamom seeds
15 black peppercorns
2 tablespoons sunflower oil
3 red onions, sliced
2 tablespoons ginger-garlic paste
300g (10oz) cooked chicken, cut into strips
Salt
1 tablespoon lemon juice

1 Dry roast the spices in a small saucepan, cool then whizz in a coffee mill to make a fine powder. Reserve.

2 Heat the sunflower oil in a wok or medium saucepan. Add half the red onions and fry until soft. Stir in the ginger-garlic paste and cook for 1 minute.

3 Add the cooked chicken and salt and heat through.

4 Mix in the reserved black spice powder and serve warm, sprinkled with the remaining onions and lemon juice, with rotis if liked.

Kolmi til Kebab

According to Ayurveda, the Indian system of holistic medicine, sesame is a warming spice that creates heat in the body and therefore it is largely eaten in the winter. Indian dishes mostly use the cream-coloured variety of sesame and in this recipe it adds a wonderful nutty taste that perfectly complements the salty, sea flavour of the prawns. Serves 4

Preparation time: 10 minutes **Cooking time:** 25 minutes

3 tablespoons white sesame seeds
300g (10oz) tiger prawns, uncooked, peeled, tails left on
1 tablespoon garlic paste
1/2 teaspoon turmeric powder
1 teaspoon red chilli flakes
Salt
Sunflower oil for shallow frying

1 Dry roast the sesame seeds in a small saucepan until they turn golden. Keep the heat low so that the seeds get cooked through. Reserve.

2 Combine the prawns, garlic, turmeric powder, chilli flakes and salt in a mixing bowl.

3 Heat the oil in a medium pan and shallow fry the prawns on both sides.

4 Remove from heat, drain the prawns and toss them in the toasted sesame seeds. Serve immediately.

CRISP STACKS OF POTATO, SWEET POTATO AND ONION

Batata Kaap

Kaap, or south Indian vegetable fritters, are always served as part of a festive meal. A variety of vegetables is used: fresh yams, bitter karelas, raw bananas or plantain and native monsoon vegetables such as controlli and parval. The fritters are deliberately made salty to counter the blandness of the vegetables, much in the way chips taste better when sprinkled liberally with salt. Serves 4

Preparation time: 15 minutes **Cooking time:** 30 minutes

1/2 teaspoon chilli powder
Salt
4 tablespoons rice flour
2 large potatoes, peeled and sliced into rounds
2 sweet potatoes, peeled and sliced into rounds
2 onions, cut into rounds
Sunflower oil for deep frying
Few fresh coriander stalks

1 Combine the chilli powder, salt and rice flour in a mixing bowl. Fold in the vegetables, evenly coating them with the spice and salt mixture.

2 Heat the oil in a deep wok or heavy-bottomed saucepan until smoking.

3 Fry the vegetables in batches until golden. This should take only about 1 minute, or they will burn. Remove with a slotted spoon and drain on kitchen paper.

4 To serve, make a stack of alternating vegetables slices – potato, sweet potato and onion. Continue until you have a reasonable stack on each individual serving plate. Serve immediately, garnished with fresh coriander.

CRISP AND SPICY CHICKPEA CANAPÉS

Channe ke Kurkure

Cosmopolitan parties in urban India are often elaborate dinners preceded by cocktails. Various canapés are served as a finger buffet with drinks, with toppings as diverse as asparagus or coriander chutney. This one is a real taste-bud teaser, with a blend of salty, spicy and tangy flavours. Serves 4

Preparation time: 10 minutes **Cooking time:** 5 minutes

1 tablespoon sunflower oil
1 teaspoon ginger-garlic paste
1 teaspoon garam masala powder
2 tablespoons tomato purée
150g (5oz) canned chickpeas, drained and rinsed
Salt
20 crostini
Few fresh coriander stalks, finely chopped

1 Heat the oil in a wok or a heavy-bottomed saucepan.

2 Fry the ginger-garlic paste for 1 minute then add the garam masala powder.

3 Stir in the tomato purée and cook for a few minutes.

4 Add the chickpeas to the pan, season with salt and heat until heated through.

5 Spoon the chickpeas on top of each crostini and serve warm, sprinkled with fresh coriander. Allow 5 per person.

Guldasta aur Bharta

This literally means a bouquet served with a smoky aubergine dip. The bouquet is a selection of fresh seasonal vegetables served raw, so that the crunch is contrasted by the smoothness of the aubergine. The dip is a very popular dish in Maharashtra and is usually eaten with rotis and a slice of raw onion. Serves 4

Preparation time: 20 minutes **Cooking time:** 45 minutes

1 large aubergine
2 tablespoons sunflower oil
1/2 teaspoon cumin seeds
1 onion, finely chopped
1 teaspoon ginger-garlic paste
1 fresh green chilli, chopped
Salt
6 tablespoons natural yogurt
300g (10oz) crunchy seasonal salad vegetables, such as carrots,
    celery sticks, mushrooms, green peppers, cucumbers

1 Brush the aubergine with some of the oil and place under a hot grill. Keep turning until cooked and the skin has turned crisp. This can take up to 30 minutes.

2 Scrape off the skin with a knife and mash the flesh of the aubergine with a fork. Reserve.

3 Heat the oil in a saucepan or wok and fry the cumin seeds until they change colour. Add the onion and fry until soft.

4 Add the ginger-garlic paste and the green chilli and fry for 1 minute.

5 Season with salt and stir in the aubergine. Mix well and remove from the heat. Allow the mixture to cool then stir in the yogurt.

6 Serve at room temperature with the salad vegetables.

Chutney Naan

This is a great vegetarian starter for a meat-rich meal. It is inspired by a very popular Bombay favourite called sev puri. However, you can make it with a meat-based topping such as the Chicken Salad with Black Spices and Red Onion (page 23) if you prefer. I usually make the chutney well in advance and assemble the dish when I am ready to serve it. Serves 4

Preparation time: 10 minutes

3 tablespoons bottled mint sauce
1 teaspoon ginger-garlic paste
1 large red tomato, finely chopped
1/4 cucumber, finely chopped
Salt
2 large naans, cut into quarters
4 tablespoons any sweet and sour Bombay mix

1 Mix the mint sauce and ginger-garlic paste in a small bowl. Reserve.

2 Mix the tomato and cucumber and season with salt. (If you are going to assemble the dish later, season it just before serving as adding salt at this stage will soften the vegetables.)

3 To serve, divide the naan between 4 individual plates, spread each piece with a little mint chutney and top with the seasoned vegetables. Sprinkle with Bombay mix and serve immediately.

In India, eggs are considered to be non vegetarian; no vegetarian will eat anything that contains eggs, such as cakes and some puddings and biscuits, so there is a high demand for the stunning array of eggless cakes offered by most bakeries and confectioners for birthday and wedding anniversary parties.

Those who do eat eggs prefer them well spiced with green chillies and freshly crushed black pepper. In many cities, street vendors sell boiled eggs in their shell as a roadside snack. There is always salt, pepper and a shaker filled with red hot chilli powder to hand.

On a more sophisticated note, the Parsees, who came to India from Persia many hundred years ago, use eggs extensively in their cooking. Parsi food is a delicious blend of Persian and Indian cuisine and is very popular in India. The Parsees serve fried eggs on top of spiced vegetables such as okra and potatoes, and serve eggs boiled and sliced over festive sweets such as semolina pudding.

Mughlai cooking from the north, which is inspired by the Islamic rulers of Delhi in centuries past, also includes eggs. Typical of their cuisine are rotis rolled in beaten egg then fried. Boiled, halved eggs are also used to garnish luxurious meat biryanis.

And of course there is that great café institution in Mumbai – the Irani restaurant, which is quite similar to the reasonably priced, quick service, high turnover cafés of the West. These eateries are run by the Iranian community who came to India over many decades. The most popular dish they serve is spiced omelette with a buttered roll. It never tastes the same at home and it really is to die for!

Eggs

Andyachi Surli

A great dish for a light lunch, this roll is a perfect combination of eggs and vegetables. Serve it with buttered bread and a green salad or with Brown Rice with Onion and Pinenuts (page 158). I use closed cup mushrooms but you could try any variety that you fancy. Serves 4

Preparation time: 10 minutes **Cooking time:** 15 minutes

6 large eggs
Salt
2 tablespoons sunflower oil
1/2 teaspoon cumin seeds
1/2 teaspoon turmeric powder
1/2 teaspoon chilli powder
500g (18oz) closed cup mushrooms, sliced
Few fresh coriander stalks, chopped

1 Beat the eggs in a bowl, season with salt and reserve.

2 Heat the oil in a frying pan and add the cumin seeds. Fry until they change colour.

3 Add the spice powders then immediately add the mushrooms. Stir until softened.

4 Remove from the heat and reserve.

5 Wipe down the pan and pour in a quarter of the beaten egg. When it turns golden on the bottom, flip it over and cook the other side. Keep warm while you make a further 3 omelettes in this way.

6 To serve, season the mushroom mixture with salt (adding salt earlier will make the mushroom mixture watery). Place an omelette on a serving plate and place a quarter of the mushroom mixture down the middle of Sprinkle with a little coriander (reserving some for garnish) and fold both the sides in to make a roll. Repeat for the other 3 omelettes.

7 Sprinkle the remaining coriander over the omelettes and serve warm.

Dimer Jhol

A typical Bengali meal consists of curry and rice. Most often this is a fish curry, using the many river fish that abound in the region. However, egg curry is also very popular and can be quite hot and fiery. Vary the chilli here to suit your own taste. Serves 4

Preparation time: 15 minutes **Cooking time:** 30 minutes

2 medium potatoes
8 large eggs, hardboiled for 10–12 minutes
3 tablespoons sunflower oil
1 onion, finely chopped
1 tablespoon ginger-garlic paste
1 teaspoon turmeric powder
1 teaspoon red chilli powder
1 teaspoon garam masala powder
Salt

1 Boil the potatoes until cooked. Drain then peel and dice the potatoes. Peel the eggs but keep them whole and reserve.

2 Heat the sunflower oil in a wok or saucepan and fry the potatoes until golden and crisp. Remove with a slotted spoon and reserve.

3 Smear the eggs with half the turmeric and fry in the same oil until brown. Remove and reserve.

4 Fry the onion until soft. Add the ginger-garlic paste and stir for 1 minute.

5 Add the spice powders and salt. Pour in 300ml (10fl oz) hot water and bring to the boil.

6 Reduce the heat and simmer for 10 minutes. Gently add the eggs and the potatoes to the curry. Serve hot.

Baida Malai Kadhi

This is another recipe that calls for hard-boiled eggs. If you keep raw and hard-boiled eggs together, one way of telling if an egg is hard boiled is to spin it. A hard-boiled egg will spin round while a semi-cooked or raw one will wobble. Also, always use the freshest eggs you can. To test for freshness put them into a deep bowl of water. Fresh eggs should sink. Egg yolks are also one of the few foods that naturally contain vitamin D. Serves 4

Preparation time: 10 minutes **Cooking time:** 30 minutes

Large eggs, hard boiled for 10–12 minutes
2 tablespoons sunflower oil
1 tablespoon ginger-garlic paste
2 tablespoons tomato purée
/2 teaspoon turmeric powder
/2 teaspoon chilli powder
450ml (1 pint) coconut milk
Fresh coriander leaves, chopped

1 Peel the eggs and halve them. Reserve.

2 Heat the sunflower oil in a wok or heavy-bottomed saucepan and fry the ginger-garlic paste for 1 minute.

3 Add the tomato purée and stir. Add the spice powders.

4 Place the eggs in the pan and baste them with the spice mixture.

5 Pour in the coconut milk and gently heat through without allowing the curry to boil.

6 Serve the hot curry garnished with chopped coriander.

Tantya Bhurji

Goa is home to a wonderful and unique cuisine. Spicy coconut gravies form the backdrop for a star-filled cast of sausages, ham, pork, all manner of seafood, and chicken. This dish has traditional Goan smoked sausages called chouricos which are quite highly spiced and salted. Chouricos are eaten in the monsoon when fish is scarce because fishing boats are unable to go out into the rough seas. Serves 4

Preparation time: 10 minutes **Cooking time:** 10 minutes

6 large eggs
Salt
2 tablespoons sunflower oil
2 green chillies, finely chopped
4 Goan or other spicy cooked sausages such as chorizo, sliced thickly
4 slices cooked ham
2 tablespoons tomato purée
1 teaspoon coriander powder

1 Beat the eggs in a large bowl, season with salt and reserve.

2 Heat the oil in a heavy-bottomed saucepan and fry the chillies.

3 Almost immediately, add the sliced sausage and fry for 1 minute.

4 Add the ham and stir well.

5 Stir in the tomato purée and coriander powder and cook until well blended for about 3 minutes.

6 Add the beaten eggs and cook over a low heat, stirring all the time to scramble them. Remove from the heat once they are nearly set and keep stirring: the pan will be hot enough to finish the cooking. The eggs should be soft and glossy.

7 Serve at once with buttered buns or rotis.

Nargisi Paratha

This bread is a meal in itself and can be served for brunch or a light lunch. The trick in this recipe is to stuff the bread correctly and this can be done by choosing the right amount of stuffing for each piece of bread. Too much will make it pop out during the cooking and too little will make the bread bland and lifeless. I also think that using ghee for this adds such an extra flavour that it's worth indulging yourself! Serves 4

Preparation time: 20 minutes   **Cooking time:** 35 minutes

2 tablespoons sunflower oil
2 green chillies, finely chopped
1/2 teaspoon turmeric powder
Salt
3 medium eggs, hard boiled for 10 minutes, peeled and mashed
3 tablespoons coriander leaves, finely chopped
450g (1lb) wholewheat flour or atta
2 tablespoons ghee

1 Heat the oil in a medium saucepan or wok and fry the green chillies for a few seconds.

2   Add the turmeric powder, season with salt and add the eggs immediately. Stir well.

3 Sprinkle in the coriander leaves and remove from the heat. Reserve this mixture.

4 Combine the atta (reserving a little for dusting the bread) and about 220ml (scant 1/2 pint) of warm water in a mixing bowl. You may need a little less or more water, depending on the quality of the flour.

5 Knead this into a stiff dough. Divide the dough into equal-sized balls the size of a small lime. You should get about 12. Smear your palms with little oil and shape the balls smoothly.

6 Flatten each ball of dough, dust with a little flour and roll into a small disc, about 5cm (2in) in diameter.

7 Place a tablespoon of the mixture into the centre of this disc and fold over the edges inwards to seal in the stuffing.

8 Gently roll out the disc to make it flat and about 12 cm (5in) in diameter. Make sure that you do not press down while rolling or the stuffing will ooze out.

9 Meanwhile, heat a griddle and when quite hot, place the rolled-out paratha on it. Dot the edges with ghee and smear some on the surface.

10 When the underside is brown, flip it over and cook the other side in the same way.

11 Keep the parathas warm in aluminium foild while you cook the rest in the same way. Serve hot with a sweet relish or a chicken dish such as the Chicken and Coconut Stir Fry (page 74).

Nargisi Kofte

This is a very traditional north Indian dish and can be eaten on its own or served in an onion gravy. In times past it was made with many different spices but with modern ready-prepared spices it is possible to make it with just a handful of ingredients. I often serve these around Easter – the kids love the surprise of splitting open the kofta to find the hidden egg within. Serves 4

Preparation time: 10 minutes **Cooking time:** 40 minutes

4 large eggs
300g (10oz) lean lamb mince
1 tablespoon ginger-garlic paste
$^1/_2$ teaspoon garam masala powder
$^1/_2$ teaspoon turmeric powder
$^1/_2$ teaspoon chilli powder
Salt
150g (5oz) breadcrumbs
Sunflower oil for deep frying

1 Hard boil and peel the eggs. Reserve.

2 Combine the mince, ginger-garlic paste, spice powders and salt. Mix well. Divide the mince into 4 portions.

3 Wrap a portion of mince around each egg to completely cover it.

4 Heat the oil in a wok or deep frying pan. When it is nearly smoking, reduce the heat. Roll each encased egg in the breadcrumbs and deep fry on low heat until well browned on all sides.

5 Serve hot with tomato ketchup (best!) or raita.

When I think of seafood in India, a picture immediately forms in my mind. When I'm in Mumbai, Sunday mornings are devoted to a special trip to the fish market. I wake the kids early (this trip is for them really!), we put on our 'fish-market shoes', take along a couple of plastic carrier bags and set off to buy fish for lunch.

The market is actually the dock where the trawlers land their early morning catch. Buyers wait for the boats and can watch the seafood being unloaded. There are many kinds of fish, long, smooth eels, as well as blue and silver crabs, fat lobsters, giant prawns, squid and shellfish. The largest fish are snapped up by the restaurant buyers who are regular customers at the docks.

The fish sellers on the dock who work closely with the boatmen begin the day's business by naming a price. We then start bargaining for our chosen fish. The dialogue in itself is an art and someone with good negotiating skills can come away with a large fresh fish for next to nothing.

The kids and I return home soon after sunrise and set about cleaning our fish and prawns. A good shower later, we begin to grind the spices for the curry that will be presented at the table for lunch. For the adults, the meal is preceded by glasses of cold lager that has been chilling for a few hours!

Fish & Shellfish

Sabut Machli Masala

This is a Goan style of cooking fish and the spicy coating goes beautifully with the fresh fish caught daily in the Arabian Sea, off the shores of Goa. It reminds me of sun-soaked holidays filled with food and lazy days on the beach. Serves 4

Preparation time: 15 minutes + 30 minutes marinating
Cooking time: 40 minutes

2 teaspoons garam masala powder
2 teaspoons chilli powder
2 teaspoons turmeric powder
4 teaspoons ginger-garlic paste
6 tablespoons malt vinegar
Salt
2 teaspoons sugar
2 whole firm fish, such as rainbow trout, well cleaned, gutted
   and scaled
Sunflower oil to shallow fry

1 Dry roast the garam masala powder in a small saucepan for just 1 minute (any longer and you may scorch the spice powder).

2 In a small bowl, combine the roasted garam masala, chilli and turmeric powders, ginger-garlic paste, vinegar, salt and sugar.

3 Smear the mixture on the fish, making sure that it is evenly coated inside and out. Allow the fish to marinate in the spices for at least 30 minutes.

4 Heat the oil in a frying pan and fry the fish on both sides until well cooked. Serve hot with a simple squeeze of lime juice and either rice or bread.

LIME-FLAVOURED CRISP PRAWNS

Khatte Jhinge

The joy of buying prawns in India is that they are only ever sold fresh, never cooked. This means that you can choose to cook them as you like and will always end up with a perfectly textured dish. Here the tang of green lime complements the natural sweet salty flavour of prawns fresh from the sea. Serves 4

Preparation time: 10 minutes **Cooking time:** 25 minutes

for the seasoning
1 teaspoon chilli powder
1 teaspoon garlic paste
Salt
2 tablespoons fresh lime juice

600g (1¼lb) large uncooked prawns, shelled
Sunflower oil for deep frying
5 tablespoons rice flour

1 Combine the ingredients for the seasoning and toss the prawns in it. Don't leave the prawns in the marinade, however, because the lime juice will begin to cook them and spoil the final texture.

2 Heat the oil in a large frying pan

3 Roll the prawns, a few at a time, in the rice flour then shake off excess flour. Fry them in the hot oil for a few minutes until crisp and golden. Remove and drain on kitchen paper and keep hot. Continue to cook all the prawns in small batches.

4 Serve hot with slices of red onion.

CRAB WITH SOUTH INDIAN SPICES

Khekda Dakshin

In India, crabs are always sold live so that you know they are fresh. My grandmother taught me to look for female crabs which have a dark triangular shell on the underside, because she believed they were fleshie She also always bought crabs closer to the day of the full moon because she said they were fuller then. Serves 4

Preparation time: 25 minutes **Cooking time:** 25 minutes

4 large cooked, prepared crabs, white meat only
2 tablespoons sunflower oil
½ teaspoon black mustard seeds
5 curry leaves
2 red chillies, stalks pinched off, seeds shaken out, broken into piece
1 teaspoon turmeric powder
1½ teaspoons ginger-garlic paste
4 tablespoons coconut, preferably freshly grated, or desiccated
Salt

1 Remove the flesh from the crabs and shred it. Reserve the shells.

2 Heat the oil in a saucepan and fry the mustard seeds until they pop.

3 Add the curry leaves and the red chillies. Sprinkle in the turmeric powder. Stir in the ginger-garlic paste.

4 Add the shredded crab to the pan and season with salt. Mix well.

5 Take the crab mixture off the heat and stir in the coconut.

6 Stuff the spiced meat back into the shells and serve warm.

Flower Sungtachi Bhaji

Many communities in India specialise in combining meat or seafood with vegetables and such dishes form a large part of their cuisine. One such community is the Goan Hindus and this is one of their recipes. The cauliflower could be substituted with green beans or cabbage. Serves 4

Preparation time: 20 minutes **Cooking time:** 30 minutes

2 tablespoons sunflower oil
1 teaspoon black mustard seeds
1 teaspoon cumin seeds
1 teaspoon ginger-garlic paste
1 teaspoon turmeric powder
1 teaspoon chilli powder
150g (5oz) uncooked shrimps, peeled
300g (10oz) cauliflower, cut into small florets
Salt

1 Heat the sunflower oil in a wok or heavy-bottomed saucepan and fry the mustard seeds until they pop. Add the cumin seeds and the ginger-garlic paste.

2 Stir and add the spice powders, shrimps and cauliflower.

3 Season with salt and mix well. Add a few tablespoons of water to the pan and reduce the heat. Cook until the cauliflower is done but firm.

4 Serve hot.

Kadhai Jhinga

In north Indian cookery, tomatoes often form the base for curries. The red of ripe tomatoes and the blazing chilli powder determine the colour of the final dish. In this recipe, green peppers add a colour contrast. Ideally, you need to cook this dish in a kadhai or Indian wok which, being heavier than the Chinese version, facilitates the even distribution of heat so that the curry does not burn. Serves 4

Preparation time: 20 minutes **Cooking time:** 20 minutes

3 tablespoons sunflower oil
1 large onion, finely chopped
1 teaspoon ginger-garlic paste
3 ripe red tomatoes, chopped
1 teaspoon turmeric powder
1 teaspoon chilli powder
1 large green pepper, de-seeded and diced
300g (10oz) large cooked prawns, peeled
Salt

1 Heat the oil in a heavy wok or kadhai and fry the onion until softened.

2 Fry the ginger-garlic paste and stir a few times.

3 Tip in the tomatoes and the spice powders and cook until the mixture is soft and mushy. Add a little water to prevent it from sticking to the pan.

4 Add the pepper and the prawns, season with salt and pour in about 150ml (5fl oz) hot water to make a thick sauce. Cook until done, adding more water as necessary.

5 Serve hot with a roti.

Khatti Meethi Machhi

first tasted this curry in my friend Geeta's house in Mumbai and fell in love with the perfect blend of flavours. The sweet and sour tastes complement the natural saltiness of the fish, and mustard brings in a burst of heat. Serve this with a fresh roti or plain boiled rice and a lentil dish such as Lentils with Spinach and Garlic (page 104). Serves 4

Preparation time: 15 minutes **Cooking time:** 30 minutes

1 tablespoon wholegrain mustard
1 teaspoon turmeric powder
Salt
firm fish steaks, such as cod, weighing 300g (10oz) in total
4 tablespoons sunflower oil
1 large onion, finely chopped
2 tablespoons tamarind pulp
1 tablespoon soft brown sugar

1 Mix the mustard, turmeric powder and salt and smear well onto the fish steaks.

2 Heat the oil in a shallow, wide saucepan and fry the spiced fish on both sides until nearly done. Remove and reserve.

3 Fry the onion in the same oil until soft. Add the tamarind pulp and the sugar and mix well. Check the seasoning and add salt if necessary.

4 When the oil separates out of the mixture, gently place the fish into the pan and finish cooking it. Serve hot, garnished with fresh coriander leaves if liked.

Bangda Ghashi

*This popular south Indian dish is the epitome of coastal cookery.
Enormous tamarind trees grow outside the homes and children can often
be seen throwing pebbles into the tree to get at the sour, pulpy fruit. The
fruit is shelled and the seeds taken out. All summer long, women roll the
pulp into balls, salt them well and preserve them for use later in the year.
Serves 4*

Preparation time: 20 minutes **Cooking time:** 20 minutes

3 tablespoons sunflower oil
1/2 teaspoon fenugreek seeds
1 teaspoon black peppercorns
5 dried red chillies, stalks pinched off, seeds shaken out
4 tablespoons desiccated coconut
1 teaspoon ginger-garlic paste
1 tablespoon tamarind pulp
2 large mackerel, cleaned and cut into thick steaks
Salt

1 Heat a tablespoon of the oil in a wok or small saucepan. Fry the
fenugreek seeds and peppercorns for a few minutes. The fenugreek
seeds should start to darken.

2 Add the red chillies and the coconut and fry until the mixture starts to
turn golden.

3 Cool the mixture and whizz in the blender with a little water until the
mixture is smooth. Reserve.

4 Wipe out the wok and heat the rest of the oil in it.

5 Fry the ginger-garlic paste for 1 minute. Stir in the tamarind pulp.

6 Place the fish in the pan and fry well on both sides. Pour in the coconut
and spice mixture, season with salt and bring to the boil. Cook on low
heat until the fish is done.

7 Serve hot with plain boiled rice.

Malvani Mori

The Arabian Sea off India's west coast yields many culinary treasures. Baby sharks are often netted and made into a wonderfully tangy curry. If you prefer, use another firm-fleshed fish, say monkfish. The skin of the shark is quite difficult to remove: a task best left to your fishmonger. Shark tastes quite rich and meaty and therefore needs to be well spiced. I like to serve this curry with a refreshing vegetable stir fry such as Gujarati-style Cabbage and Carrot (page 93). Serves 4

Preparation time: 20 minutes **Cooking time:** 40 minutes

tablespoons sunflower oil
large onion, finely chopped
teaspoon ginger-garlic paste
tablespoons freshly grated, or desiccated coconut
300g (10oz) shark meat or monkfish, cubed
1/2 teaspoon chilli powder
tablespoon garam masala powder
1/2 tablespoons tamarind pulp
salt

1 Heat 1 tablespoon of the oil in a wok or shallow saucepan. Fry half the onion until soft. Add the ginger-garlic paste and the coconut and fry until the mixture is well browned.

2 Whizz the mixture in a blender, adding a little water, to form a fine paste. Reserve.

3 Heat the remaining oil in another wok or heavy-bottomed saucepan and fry the remaining onion until soft. Add the shark meat. Stir until well sealed on all sides and mix in the spice powders.

4 Pour in the reserved coconut mixture and the tamarind pulp. Season with salt and add a few tablespoons of water. Cook until the fish is done and serve hot with rice. The curry should be semi liquid with the sauce coating the fish.

Mahi Mirch Kabab

These fishcakes make a great light lunch or even a picnic meal. They can be put into a bun with some crunchy salad leaves and a relish such as the Hot Tomato Relish (page 150). I have made these with prawns instead of fish and they work just as well. Serves 4

Preparation time: 15 minutes **Cooking time:** 40 minutes

300g (10oz) firm fish fillets, such as cod
Sunflower oil to shallow fry
1 onion, finely chopped
1 teaspoon ginger-garlic paste
2 fresh green chillies, finely chopped
1 teaspoon turmeric powder
Salt
4 slices of white bread, crusts removed
3 tablespoons semolina

1 Poach the fish in some salted water. Drain and flake the flesh. Reserve.

2 Heat a couple of tablespoons of oil in a shallow saucepan and fry the onion until soft. Add the ginger-garlic paste and the green chillies.

3 Sprinkle in the turmeric powder, give it a good stir and remove from the heat.

4 Tip this onion mixture into a mixing bowl. Season with salt and add the bread. Knead well until it resembles a dough.

5 Gently fold the fish into the dough. Make little balls of the dough, each the size of a lime. Flatten and reserve.

6 Heat the oil in a shallow saucepan. Roll the fishcakes in semolina, shake off the excess and fry on both sides until golden brown. Serve hot.

Paneer Jhinga

Some communities in India believe that dairy products should not be mixed with seafood, although countless recipes with such combinations exist. Many people say that it is pure milk that is not to be combined because milk and seafood work in contrasting ways on the digestion. Paneer is quite firm in texture and will hold its shape if treated gently. It softens on cooking, giving a nice spongy feel to the dish. Serves 4

Preparation time: 15 minutes **Cooking time:** 10 minutes

2 tablespoons sunflower oil
2 teaspoons ginger-garlic paste
3 tablespoons tomato purée
4 fresh green chillies, slit down the middle
300g (10oz) cooked large prawns, peeled or unpeeled
1 teaspoon turmeric powder
Salt
100g (3¹/₂oz) paneer (Indian cottage cheese), cubed
100ml (3¹/₂fl oz) single cream

1 Heat the oil in a saucepan and fry the ginger-garlic paste for 1 minute.

2 Add the tomato purée and 2 of the chillies and cook until the oil separates, adding a couple of tablespoons of water to hasten the process.

3 Tip in the prawns, turmeric powder and salt. Mix well and cook for a few minutes until everything is well blended.

4 Fold in the paneer quite gently and pour in the cream. Heat through without allowing to boil.

5 Serve immediately, garnished with the remaining 2 green chillies.

India has many vegetarian people and those who do eat meat also follow strict rules about their diet. The Hindus, who make up most of the population, do not eat beef for religious reasons. They worship the cow as a sacred animal and will not kill one. The Muslims do not eat pork, also for religious reasons. This is why most restaurants in India serve only lamb and chicken dishes. Even some international fast food chains that have established themselves in many Indian cities have had to make it very clear to the public that there is no beef or pork on their menu.

In India, the meat called mutton is goat flesh. In the north, especially in the hilly regions of Kashmir, sheep meat is preferred and the cooking is done in sheep's fat.

In days gone by, when India still had princely states and hunting was not a banned sport, the Maharajas who ruled these states would hunt in their forests, accompanied by special game cooks who were required to serve up feasts of venison, wild boar and peacock. The meat was always cooked in lots of ghee with a long list of spices used to make rich curry sauces. Many of the recipes still exist but would be viewed as unhealthy by modern diet-conscious standards.

In most homes today, mutton is eaten in the form of curries, kebabs and patties. It is cooked with rice to make fragrant pulaos and biryanis and is sometimes pickled with hot spices to add a zing to an everyday meal.

Meat

Elaichi Gosht Kebab

Although this could be cooked on a barbecue, I find it does equally well in the oven, finished off under a hot grill. It can be quite a dramatic party dish and goes well with a creamy raita. Serve it on a bed of South Indian Rice Flavoured with Lemon and Cashew Nuts (page 158) and Monsoon Salad (page 116) for great colour. Serves 4

Preparation time: 15 minutes + 1 hour marinating
Cooking time: 1 hour

2 onions
2 teaspoons ginger-garlic paste
150ml (5fl oz) natural yogurt
1 teaspoon chilli powder
1 teaspoon turmeric powder
1 teaspoon powdered cardamom seeds
600g (11/4lb) lean lamb, cubed
Salt
3 tablespoons sunflower oil

Wooden skewers

1 Roughly chop one of the onions. Cut the second into large chunks and reserve.

2 Grind the chopped onion, ginger-garlic paste and the yogurt in a blender until you get a fine paste.

3 Mix in the chilli and turmeric powders and the powdered cardamom into the onion mixture. Marinate the lamb in this for 1 hour.

4 Heat the oven to 220°C/425°F/gas 6. Thread the meat and the reserved onion chunks alternately onto the skewers.

5 Place the skewers into a greased baking tray and drizzle with the oil.

6 Cook until the meat is tender. Finish off under a hot grill for a slightly charred effect.

Kheema Ke Samose

Samosas are very popular all over the world and can be served as a snack, a main meal or a picnic treat. My kids love these for tea. In India, they are served with tomato ketchup, sweet and sour tamarind chutney or a spicy mint relish. They can be filled with a variety of stuffings – chicken mince, peas and potatoes or even mixed vegetables. Although they are traditionally deep fried, I bake my samosas for a healthier option.
Serves 4

Preparation time: 15 minutes **Cooking time**: 1 hour

2 tablespoons sunflower oil
1 onion, finely chopped
1 tablespoon ginger-garlic paste
1/2 teaspoon turmeric powder
1 teaspoon garam masala powder
300g (10oz) lean lamb mince
150g (5oz) frozen garden peas
Salt
500g (18oz) fresh ready to use filo pastry, cut into strips 10.5cm wide

1 Heat the oil in a wok or heavy-bottomed saucepan and sauté the onions until soft. Add the ginger-garlic paste and stir.

2 Add the spice powders and mix well.

3 Stir in the mince and cook until it changes colour.

4 Add the peas and salt and cook until the mince and the peas are done

5 Line a baking tray with aluminium foil and heat the oven to 220°C/425°F/gas 6.

6 Lay a sheet of pastry on a flat surface. Fill with a little of the mince and peas mixture. Fold the pastry to make a triangle, seal the edges, and continue similarly with the rest of the mince to make 12 samosas.

7 Bake in the pre-heated oven for 25–30 minutes, turning over once to cook both sides. Serve hot.

Maans Anjeer

North Indian cooking often combines dried or fresh fruit and nuts with meat or chicken to produce dishes that are a blend of flavours and textures. In India, dried figs are sold strung onto slim ropes made from straw and are quite expensive. Fresh figs are cheaper and are more easily available. This recipe works well with fresh figs but you could try the dried ones at a pinch. Serves 4

Preparation time: 10 minutes + 15 minutes marinating
Cooking time: 1 hour

1 large onion, sliced
2 teaspoons ginger-garlic paste
600g (1¼lb) lean lamb, cubed
4 tablespoons sunflower oil
1 teaspoon turmeric powder
1 teaspoon chilli powder
Salt
150ml (5fl oz) natural yogurt
6 fresh figs, 5 halved and 1 reserved for garnish

1 Whizz the onion and the ginger-garlic in a blender to make a fine paste. In a large bowl, mix the paste with the lamb and marinate for 15 minutes.

2 Heat the oil in a heavy-bottomed saucepan and fry the meat, stirring it around to prevent it from sticking.

3 When the meat is well sealed on all sides, sprinkle in the spice powders and salt. Mix well and pour in about 150ml (5fl oz) hot water. Bring the curry to a sizzle, then cover the pan and reduce the heat. Add more water as necessary to keep the curry moist and to cook the meat.

4 When the meat is nearly cooked add the yogurt and the figs. Cover and cook until the meat is done and the figs are pulpy.

5 Serve hot, garnished with the reserved fig.

MINTED ROAST LAMB

Pudina Raan

A raan (roast) is quite a festive dish and can be served at a formal dinner. It is associated with Kashmiri cooking and is often made in clay ovens like the tandoor. One of the finest raans I have tasted was cooked by Richard Holkar, current Maharaja of the royal family of Indore, for a New Year's Eve banquet at his very elegant palace in Maheshwar, in central India.

Preparation time: 15 minutes

Cooking time: about 1¼ hours, depending on size and quality of leg

½ leg of lamb, fillet end
Salt
2 teaspoons fennel seed powder
4 teaspoons ginger-garlic paste
Large handful mint leaves
2 tablespoons lemon juice
3 teaspoons garam masala powder
2 tablespoons ghee

1 Make 6–8 incisions in the meat and rub with salt. Reserve.

2 Put the fennel seed powder, ginger-garlic paste, mint leaves, lemon juice and garam masala powder in a small blender and whizz until smooth.

3 Smear the meat with this spiced mint purée. Place the meat in a greased roasting tin with a knob of ghee and cook in a pre-heated oven at 190°C/375°F/gas 5 for 30 minutes per pound.

4 When the lamb is well cooked, transfer it to a serving dish, drain off the fat and collect the juices to serve with the 'raan'. Serve this with Kashmiri Walnut Chutney (page 150) and hot rotis.

DELHI-STYLE LAMB WITH FRESH SPINACH

Delhi Saag Gosht

There is something quite special about tender lamb pieces in a creamy spinach sauce: this is a recipe from north India. One of the best Saag Goshts I have ever eaten was cooked for me by my friend Chef Avinash in Mumbai. The meat was so tender it almost melted into the spinach and the flavour was fresh and yet quite rich. Serves 4

Preparation time: 15 minutes **Cooking time:** 45 minutes

400g (14oz) fresh spinach, washed, drained and chopped
3 tablespoons sunflower oil
1 large onion, finely chopped
3 teaspoons ginger-garlic paste
2 green chillies, finely chopped
1 teaspoon powdered allspice
600g (1¼lb) lean lamb, cubed
Salt
3 teaspoons lemon juice

1 Cook the spinach in a little water, in an uncovered saucepan until tender. Cool and blend to a purée in a blender. Reserve.

2 Heat the oil in a heavy-bottomed saucepan and fry the onion until soft.

3 Add the ginger-garlic paste and the green chillies. Stir for a few seconds.

4 Sprinkle in the allspice and add the lamb. Stir well to prevent it from sticking. Cook until the meat is well seared on all sides.

5 Season with salt and pour in the puréed spinach. Bring to a bubble and reduce the heat. Cover and simmer until the lamb is tender.

Chandi Kalia

Awadh is the ancient name for Lucknow in north India. The distinct cuisine here, called 'Awadhi', was created for the ruling Nawabs of royal India and is known for its delicate flavours and slow cooking. Here is an updated version of an old royal recipe. I often serve this at dinner parties, with some soft rotis and a juicy tomato salad. Silver leaf or varq is available in most large Indian grocery shops. Serves 4

Preparation time: 15 minutes **Cooking time:** 1¼ hours

3 tablespoons sunflower oil
600g (1¼lb) lean lamb, cubed
2 onions, sliced
3 tablespoons ginger-garlic paste
2 tablespoons garam masala powder
150ml (5fl oz) natural yogurt
Salt
100ml (3½fl oz) double cream
1 sheet silver leaf

1 Heat the oil in a heavy-bottomed pan and fry the lamb until brown on all sides, stirring so that it does not stick to the pan.

2 Tip in the onions, ginger-garlic paste and garam masala powder and stir well. Fry until the onions turn golden.

3 Pour in the yogurt, season with salt and add 150ml (5fl oz) hot water. Cover and bring to a bubble. Reduce the heat and cook on low heat until the meat is tender, adding a little more water if the curry dries up.

4 Lift out the meat with a slotted spoon and reserve. Strain the curry then return the meat to the sauce. Add the cream. Heat through gently and serve topped with silver leaf.

Gosht Narangi

Lamb meets the tangy sweetness of oranges in this aromatic curry. The garam masala adds rich flavours and the onions are fried to add sweetness and fragrance. Most people even in India now buy ready-made garam masala powder and any reputable brand should give good results. Do use up spices and spice powders within about six months and store them in a clean dry jar, away from light. Serves 4

Preparation time: 15 minutes **Cooking time:** 1 hour

600g (1¼lb) lean lamb, cut into strips
3 teaspoons ginger-garlic paste
1 teaspoon turmeric powder
1 teaspoon garam masala powder
4 tablespoons sunflower oil
2 large onions, finely sliced
1 large orange, one half segmented, the other roughly mashed
Salt
Fresh coriander sprigs

1 Combine the lamb, ginger-garlic paste and spice powders in a large mixing bowl. Reserve.

2 Heat 2 tablespoons of the oil in a wok or a heavy-bottomed saucepan and fry the sliced onions, stirring until they are all evenly golden in colour. Drain and remove with a slotted spoon onto a sheet of kitchen paper.

3 Divide the onions into 2 equal portions, reserving 1 tablespoonful for the garnish. Grind one portion to a fine paste in a blender.

4 Add the rest of the oil to the pan and heat. Add the lamb with the spices to the pan and fry well to sear the meat on all sides.

5 Mix in the remaining portion of fried onions, the orange segments and the mashed orange along with all its juice.

6 Season with salt and pour in 150ml (5fl oz) hot water. Bring to the boil, cover the pan and reduce the heat. Cook until the meat is tender.

7 Serve hot, garnished with the reserved fried onions and the fresh coriander sprigs.

LAMB MINCE WITH TAMARIND AND COCONUT

Imli Kheema

This south Indian recipe calls for tamarind which I tend to buy in jars as ready tamarind pulp. The whole spices in this recipe cannot be substituted with spice powders as the taste will be completely different and a bit bland. Serve this dish with a roti and Wild Mango and Mustard Salad (page 116). Serves 4

Preparation time: 10 minutes   **Cooking time:** 45 minutes

3 tablespoons sunflower oil
1 teaspoon cumin seeds
1 teaspoon coriander seeds
4 dried red chillies, stalks pinched off, seeds shaken out
2 tablespoons desiccated coconut
3 teaspoons ginger-garlic paste
600g (1¼lb) lean lamb mince
2 teaspoons tamarind pulp
Salt

1 Heat 1 tablespoon of the oil in a small saucepan and add the cumin and coriander seeds. As they begin to change colour, add the red chillies and the coconut. Stir until the mixture starts to turn brown. Remove from the heat, cool and whizz in a blender until finely blended. Reserve.

2 Heat the remaining oil in a heavy-bottomed saucepan and fry the ginger-garlic paste for 1 minute.

3 Add the lamb mince and stir until it changes colour.

4 Sprinkle in the coconut and spice powder, add the tamarind pulp and season with salt. Cover and cook on a low heat until the meat is done. Serve hot.

SPICY LAMB CHOPS

Chaamp Lajawab

This recipe makes a wonderful main course, served with some rotis and a crunchy onion and lime salad. The chops will be more tender if you marinate them overnight. In India, many cooks marinade meat in mashed raw papaya to tenderise it. You could cook these chops on a barbecue during the summer – the slightly charred effect is delightful. I like to serve them with Mint and Tamarind Chutney (page 151). Serves 4

Preparation time: 10 minutes + overnight marinating
Cooking time: 1 hour

8 lamb chops
3 teaspoons ginger-garlic paste
½ teaspoon finely crushed black peppercorns
1 teaspoon cumin seeds, dry roasted and ground to a powder
1 teaspoon chilli powder
150ml (5fl oz) natural yogurt
Salt
3 tablespoons ghee

1 Combine the chops, ginger-garlic paste, peppercorns, spice powders, yogurt and salt in a mixing bowl and marinate overnight in the refrigerator.

2 Place the chops under a hot grill, turning them to cook evenly and basting frequently with the ghee.

3 Serve immediately.

4 Remove from the heat, stir in the lemon juice and serve hot with rice or rotis, garnished with mint leaves, if liked.

Chiristav Ghassi

I remember going on a picnic with friends to a beach in Goa and meeting a portly lady who said she would make us the best Goan curry we had ever tasted. While we enjoyed the sun and the sea, she went to her home nearby and returned at lunchtime with this curry. Now, when I make it, I can still feel the sea breeze through my hair as we ate al fresco under the coconut palms. Serves 4

Preparation time: 15 minutes **Cooking time:** 1½ hours

600g (1¼lb) lean pork, cubed
1 teaspoon turmeric powder
Salt
1 large onion, sliced
2 teaspoons ginger-garlic paste
10 red chillies, stalks pinched off, seeds shaken out, soaked for a few
   minutes in hot water, plus 2–3 whole ones for garnish
1 tablespoon garam masala powder
75ml (3fl oz) brown vinegar
3 tablespoons sunflower oil

1 Mix the pork, turmeric and salt in a large mixing bowl and reserve while you prepare the curry paste.

2 Whizz the onion, ginger-garlic paste, chillies, garam masala and vinegar in a blender until very finely mixed to a paste.

3 Heat the oil in a medium, heavy-bottomed saucepan and fry the pork, stirring to prevent it from sticking. Add a few teaspoons of water if the meat starts to stick.

4 Add the blended curry paste and stir to blend. Check the seasoning. Pour in enough hot water to make a pouring consistency and bring to the boil. Reduce the heat, cover the pan and cook until the pork is tender.

5 Serve hot, garnished with a few whole red chillies. Enjoy with plain boiled rice.

Non-vegetarian Indians love chicken and every region has scores of distinct recipes. Chicken is mostly cooked without its skin and is quite liberally flavoured with ginger and garlic.

In India, frozen as well as fresh chicken is available. In many places, you can choose a bird from amongst a live flock and the poultry seller will take it to a backroom and kill and dress it for you. That's fresh!

The favourite restaurant dish Chicken Tikka Masala which seems to be loved by everyone outside of India is equally popular in India, as is the robust, lemon-drizzled Tandoori Chicken. As a child growing up in Bombay (as Mumbai used to be called), I remember a speciality restaurant called Chicken Centre quite close to where we lived. Their frequently changing menu introduced me to a dazzling array of chicken delicacies from all over the country from quite an early age!

Duck is not a popular meat and tends to be eaten in places like Goa where there is a large Christian population. Quail and pheasant are considered exotic and few people eat them. Turkey is not seen regularly although it becomes available in a few cities, in select shops around Christmastime.

Many Indians do not eat meat and poultry for one month every year during the monsoon season. This is the most sacred month of the Hindu calendar and a vegetarian diet is considered 'pure' and therefore appropriate.

Poultry

CHICKEN AND COCONUT STIR FRY

Naralachi Komdi

A wonderfully simple but fragrant dish from coastal India. You could serve it as a simple lunch with any bread or as a picnic-basket filler. It is a dry dish, with the chicken coated in spiced coconut. My kids like to mix this into plain, boiled rice to eat with Peas in Saffron-Flavoured Yogurt (page 98). Serves 4

Preparation time: 10 minutes   **Cooking time:** 25 minutes

3 tablespoons sunflower oil
1 large onion, sliced
2 teaspoons ginger-garlic paste
2 fresh green chillies, finely chopped
1 teaspoon turmeric powder
600g (1¼lb) chicken breast, cut into small pieces
Salt
3 tablespoons desiccated coconut

1 Heat the sunflower oil in a heavy-bottomed saucepan and add the onion. Fry until soft.

2 Add the ginger-garlic paste and the green chillies and stir for a few seconds.

3 Tip in the turmeric powder and the chicken. Season with salt. Mix well and pour in a few tablespoons of hot water to prevent the chicken from sticking.

4 Cover the pan and cook the chicken until it is done. Stir in the coconut, heat through and serve immediately.

CHICKEN WITH TOMATO AND FRESH CORIANDER

Murgh ka Bharta

This refreshing chicken recipe from north India can be served with rotis and a crunchy green salad. I use the freshest, ripest tomatoes I can find for this dish as they add not just a juicy bite but also great colour. You could make it with strips of cooked lamb. Serves 4

Preparation time: 10 minutes   **Cooking time:** 30 minutes

3 tablespoons sunflower oil
1 large onion, sliced
2 teaspoons ginger-garlic paste
2 green chillies, chopped
3 ripe red tomatoes, cut into quarters, 1 reserved for garnish
1 teaspoon turmeric powder
Salt
600g (1¼lb) cooked chicken breast, shredded
Few sprigs fresh coriander

1 Heat the oil in a wok or a shallow saucepan.

2 Fry the onion until soft and then add the ginger-garlic paste and the green chillies.

3 Tip in 2 of the quartered tomatoes along with their juice and cook, stirring frequently, until a little mushy.

4 Add the turmeric powder and season with salt.

5 Stir in the cooked chicken and heat through. Serve immediately, garnished with the reserved tomato quarters and coriander sprigs.

Kozhi Moilee

Kerala is fondly known as God's own country, a land rich in spices, coconut palms, golden beaches, learning and literature. A traditional Kerala meal comprises many components all eaten together, served on a banana leaf. The wedding feast of the Malyalis, as the people of Kerala are called, is not to be missed. Although Kerala cookery prefers coconut oil I have used sunflower oil here, as a healthier option. Serves 4

Preparation time: 10 minutes   **Cooking time:** 25 minutes

3 tablespoons sunflower oil
1 large onion, finely chopped
2 teaspoons ginger-garlic paste
3 green chillies, chopped
2 ripe red tomatoes, chopped
6 fresh curry leaves, plus a few for garnish
600g (1¼lb) chicken breast, diced
Salt
300ml (10fl oz) canned coconut milk

1 Heat the sunflower oil in a wok or a heavy-bottomed saucepan. Fry the onion until soft and add the ginger-garlic paste.

2 Add the chillies and the tomatoes and stir until mushy.

3 Sprinkle in the curry leaves. Add the chicken and stir until sealed on all sides. Season with salt.

4 Pour in the coconut milk and bring to almost boiling point.

5 Reduce the heat and simmer until the chicken is cooked.

6 Serve hot, garnished with a few curry leaves.

Nawabi Murgh

Hyderabad in the southern state of Andhra Pradesh has had a royal past and boasts a well-developed, regal cuisine. The last ruler of this prosperous region, home to the famous Golconda mines where the Koh-i-Noor diamond was found, was the Nizam and he was, in his time, reputed to be the richest man in the world. His kitchens produced a delicate and flavoursome repertoire of dishes that are still popular today. Serves 4

Preparation time: 10 minutes   **Cooking time:** 45 minutes

Handful cashew nuts, unsalted
1 teaspoon cumin seeds
3 tablespoons sunflower oil
1 large onion, finely chopped
2 teaspoons ginger-garlic paste
600g (1¼lb) chicken breast, cut into small pieces
1 teaspoon garam masala powder
salt
150ml (5fl oz) natural yogurt

1 Soak the cashew nuts in 150ml (5fl oz) hot water for 10 minutes, leaving a few unsoaked for garnish.

2 Meanwhile, dry roast the cumin seeds in a small saucepan until they darken and become brittle. Grind them to a powder in a small blender or a coffee mill. Reserve.

3 In the same blender, purée the cashew nuts with their soaking water. Reserve.

4 Heat the oil in a wok or a heavy-bottomed saucepan and fry the onion until well browned.

5 Add the ginger-garlic paste and stir. Mix in the chicken breast and stir to seal on all sides.

6 Sprinkle in the garam masala powder and the reserved cumin powder and season with salt.

7 Add the puréed cashew nuts and pour in about 150ml (5fl oz) hot water. Beat the yogurt lightly and add to the pan. Bring to the boil. Reduce the heat, cover and simmer until the chicken is cooked.

8 Serve hot, garnished with the reserved cashew nuts and sprinkle with freshly chopped coriander leaves, if liked.

SOUTH INDIAN CHICKEN AND POTATO STEW

Kozhi Kadhi

TANDOORI-STYLE BAKED RED CHICKEN

Tandoori Murgh

Stews are made in many parts of India and served with noodles or bread. They are simple to make, lightly spiced and very flavourful. I sometimes use baking potatoes in this dish to give a slightly buttery texture. You could add peas and carrots if you like. I have tasted similar stews made with plantain or raw banana, yams and red pumpkin. Quite delicious! Serves 4

Preparation time: 10 minutes **Cooking time:** 45 minutes

25g (1oz) butter
10 black peppercorns, half of them roughly crushed
1 onion, chopped
150g (5oz) chicken breast, cubed
150g (5oz) potatoes, peeled and cubed
Salt
300ml (10fl oz) coconut milk
2 tablespoons fresh coriander leaves, finely chopped

1 Heat the butter in a shallow saucepan and add the 5 whole peppercorns. Add in the onion and allow to soften.

2 Tip in the chicken and the potatoes and stir well to sear.

3 Season with salt and pour in about 150ml (5fl oz) hot water. Bring to the boil, reduce the heat and simmer until the chicken and potatoes are almost cooked.

4 Pour in the coconut milk and gently heat through until the chicken and potatoes are done.

5 Remove from the heat and stir in the crushed peppercorns. Serve hot, sprinkled with the chopped coriander.

Tandoori cooking is possibly the most popular style of Indian cooking outside of India. Traditionally, tandoori referred to a dish cooked in a clay oven called the tandoor. However, today it may mean the spice mixture associated with these dishes. Tandoori spice powder or prepared paste, a combination of spices, salt and red colouring, is readily available. Serves 4

Preparation time: 10 minutes **Cooking time:** 45 minutes

2 teaspoons ginger-garlic paste
2 teaspoons tandoori spice powder
150ml (5fl oz) natural yogurt
8 large chicken drumsticks
2 tablespoons sunflower oil

1 Combine the ginger-garlic paste, tandoori spice powder and yogurt in a large mixing bowl.

2 Add the chicken drumsticks and mix well.

3 Heat the oven to 190°C/375°F/gas 5. Line a baking tray with aluminium foil and place the coated drumsticks on it. Drizzle with the oil.

4 Bake the chicken for 45 minutes or so, turning a couple of times and basting with the cooking juices.

5 Finish off under a hot grill if you like a slightly charred effect.

6 Serve hot, garnished with onion rings and slices of lemon.

Murgh Ki Roti

This is a dish from my teenage years. There was a wonderful street stall outside my college in Mumbai, when it was still called Bombay, that sold these 'frankies'. On the shop front was a picture of a glamorous woman in a mini skirt eating one, an image which gave the clear message that it was young, cool and hip to order one! Every other day we had a lunchtime frankie with a cold Coke and at the time it was our idea of culinary heaven! You will need rotis that are thin enough to roll so substituting these with naans or parathas will not work. For a stylish presentation, secure each roll with a strip of banana leaf. Serves 4

Preparation time: 10 minutes   **Cooking time:** 30 minutes

6 tablespoons white vinegar
4 fresh green or red chillies, finely chopped
2 tablespoons sunflower oil
2 onions, sliced finely
2 teaspoons ginger-garlic paste
1 teaspoon turmeric powder
600g (1¼lb) cooked chicken breast, shredded
Salt
4 shop-bought rotis

1 Combine the vinegar and half the chillies in a small glass bowl and reserve.

2 Heat the oil in a wok or medium saucepan and fry half the onions until soft. Reserve the other half of the onions for the garnish.

3 Add the ginger-garlic paste, the remaining chillies and the turmeric powder. Mix well.

4 Stir in the cooked chicken breast and season with salt.

5 Place one of the rotis on a serving plate. Divide the chicken mixture into four portions. Spoon one portion down the centre of the rotis. Drizzle with some of the reserved chilli–vinegar mixture to include a few chopped chillies.

6 Sprinkle some of the reserved, chopped raw onion on top and fold the roti to make a roll. Make the remaining rotis up in a similar way and serve immediately.

Reshmi Murgh

Many dishes in India still carry English names, a legacy left behind by the Raj. It is not uncommon to go to a restaurant and order say, a Chicken Lollipop, which is in actual fact chicken wings. This curry uses amchoor or mango powder, which adds a pleasant sharpness to the dish. It is made by drying tart green mangoes and then powdering them for easy storage. Amchoor is available for all Indian grocers. Serves 4

Preparation time: 10 minutes **Cooking time:** 25 minutes

2 tablespoons sunflower oil
2 teaspoons ginger-garlic paste
2 fresh green chillies, finely chopped
1 teaspoon garam masala powder
1 teaspoon amchoor (mango powder)
600g (1¼lb) chicken breast, cut into small pieces
Salt
150ml (5fl oz) double cream
3 tablespoons fresh coriander leaves, finely chopped

1 Heat the oil in a wok or heavy-bottomed saucepan and fry the ginger-garlic paste for a few seconds.

2 Reduce the heat and add the green chillies and the spice powders.

3 Quickly add the chicken or the spices will burn. Turn the heat back to high and stir the chicken to seal it well on all sides.

4 Pour in 150ml (5fl oz) hot water, season with salt and allow to cook on a low heat until the chicken is done. Add more water as necessary to make a rich curry.

5 Stir in the cream and heat through.

6 Serve hot, sprinkled with the chopped coriander. This goes well with rice or with noodles.

Dalchini Murgh

Cinnamon is most commonly available as quills but it is not too difficult to find powdered cinnamon. I would suggest you buy this spice in very small quantities as it loses its flavour quite quickly. Cinnamon is an essential part of garam masala, a mixture of warming spices that is used to flavour many north Indian savoury dishes and curries. Its sweet, woody scent is also used to enliven many desserts. *Serves 4*

Preparation time: 10 minutes **Cooking time:** 35 minutes

2 tablespoons sunflower oil
2 bay leaves
1 onion, sliced finely
2 teaspoons ginger-garlic paste
1 large tomato, chopped
600g (1¼lb) chicken drumsticks, skinned
1 teaspoon powdered cinnamon
Salt
300ml (10fl oz) coconut milk

1 Heat the oil in a wok or heavy pan. Add the bay leaves and watch for them to change colour. As soon as they do, add the onion and allow to soften.

2 Stir in the ginger-garlic paste and cook for a few seconds.

3 Tip in the tomato and cook until well blended and slightly mushy.

4 Mix in the chicken, stirring to sear well on all sides. Sprinkle in half the cinnamon and season with salt. Pour in about 150ml (5fl oz) hot water. Cover the wok and bring the curry to a boil. Reduce the heat and simmer until the chicken is cooked.

5 Pour in the coconut milk and heat through.

6 Serve hot, dusted with the rest of the cinnamon.

Puli Bathak

Duck is not a very popular bird all over India but many Christian families rear their own ducks for the dinner table. Duck meat is rich in taste and is complemented by the sweet and sour curry in this recipe. In the south, curry leaves give a distinctive flavour to most curries and the fresher these are, the better the taste. The leaves are rarely eaten but keep them in for their attractive colour. *Serves 4*

Preparation time: 10 minutes   **Cooking time:** 25 minutes

1 teaspoon turmeric powder
1 teaspoon chilli powder
3 tablespoons sunflower oil
6 fresh curry leaves
2 teaspoons ginger-garlic paste
2 tablespoons tamarind pulp
2 tablespoons soft brown sugar
Salt
600g (1¼lb) cooked duck breast, shredded

1 Combine the spice powders with a few tablespoons of water and set aside.

2 Heat the oil in a wok or a heavy-bottomed saucepan and fry the curry leaves for a couple of seconds.

3 Add the ginger-garlic paste and stir. Add the tamarind pulp, brown sugar, salt and a couple more tablespoons of water. Allow the mixture to blend well.

4 Pour in the spice powders mixed with the water and allow to cook. Add the duck and about 300ml (10fl oz) hot water to make a sauce.

5 Bring to the boil, reduce the heat and simmer for about 2 minutes. Remove from the heat and serve hot with rice or with Watermelon Pancakes (page 154).

India's variety of fresh vegetables is mind-boggling. From the many kinds of leaves including colocasia and fenugreek to the assortment of gourds, there is an arresting array in every Indian market.

These days it is not difficult to find some of these vegetables in western markets. Crisp green okra (which needs a bit of acid in the cooking to get rid of its sliminess) is seen in many places. I have also found bitter gourds (also called bitter melon or karela) in some outlets in the West. These need to be soaked in salted water for a while to lessen their bitterness. Drumstick, a long hard vegetable with a soft interior which is used in south Indian cookery, is also available in Indian shops.

The great repertoire of vegetables has meant that India has a vast vegetarian cuisine. Most Indian homes serve some vegetable dishes, even if the main course is a meat curry. This could be in the form of a stir fry, a yogurt-based raita or as a combination of vegetables and lentils.

Vegetarian cookery also includes dairy products. Paneer or Indian cottage cheese is available commercially in a slab. Homemade paneer is quite delicious and rather different to the one available in most shops. We often make it at home by curdling fresh milk with a bit of lemon juice and draining off the whey. The milk solids are pressed under a weight to firm them up and this is used as paneer.

Vegetarian

Kaddu ki Kadhi

The sweet smoothness of the pumpkin is complemented by the creaminess of the coconut milk in this divine recipe. Garlic and chilli add a bit of zing to this rather bland but very nutritious vegetable. I always keep the skin of pumpkin on as it helps hold the flesh together while it is cooking and softens enough to eat in the final dish. I love this curry with rice and hot mango pickle. Serves 4

Preparation time: 10 minutes **Cooking time:** 15 minutes

3 tablespoons sunflower oil
1 teaspoon cumin seeds
$^1/_2$ teaspoon fenugreek seeds
2 dried red chillies, left whole
300g (10 oz) red pumpkin, cut into cubes, skin on
Salt
300ml (10fl oz) coconut milk
3 garlic cloves

1 Heat 2 tablespoons of the oil in a large, heavy-bottomed pan and fry the cumin seeds for 1 minute until they darken.

2 Add the fenugreek seeds and allow them to darken. This will take only a few seconds. Drop in the red chillies.

3 Add the pumpkin and season with salt. Stir well and allow to cook, adding a little water to soften the pumpkin. When the pumpkin is soft but not mashed, pour in the coconut milk. Heat through and remove from the heat.

4 Bash the cloves of garlic once in a mortar, leaving the skin on so that it holds its shape.

5 Heat the rest of the oil in a small pan and fry the garlic until it turns golden. Pour the garlic and the oil into the pumpkin curry and serve hot.

Suva Palak ki Subji

Dill leaves are often combined with other greens to add a refreshing taste that goes well with rice and lentils. This dish can be made by adding soft vegetables such as carrots and aubergines to the mixture to make it more nutritious. It goes well with Tomato Rice with Mustard Seed (page 158). Serves 4

Preparation time: 10 minutes **Cooking time:** 30 minutes

300g (10oz) fresh spinach leaves, washed and drained
50g (2oz) fresh dill leaves, washed and drained
3 tablespoons sunflower oil
1 teaspoon cumin seeds
1 large onion, chopped finely
2 tablespoons ginger-garlic paste
2 fresh tomatoes, chopped
2 fresh green chillies, finely chopped
Salt

1 Chop the spinach and dill separately and reserve.

2 Heat the oil in a heavy-bottomed pan and fry the cumin seeds for about 1 minute until they darken.

3 Add the onion and fry until soft for about 5 minutes.

4 Stir in the ginger-garlic paste and the tomatoes. Cook until soft. Add the chillies.

5 Drop in the chopped leaves and stir well. Pour in about 150ml (5 floz) water. Season with salt. Bring to the boil, then reduce the heat and cook uncovered until the vegetables are cooked, say about 10 minutes.

6 Remove from the heat and work a hand blender through the mixture to make it into a rough purée.

7 Serve hot.

Aloo Mutter Jeerawala

The combination of potatoes and peas is a universal favourite. In India, every region has its own special recipe which is often served with poories or fried bread. In this version, common to most of India, the cumin adds a lovely warm taste. Dry roasting cumin really enhances its flavour. It then becomes quite brittle and can be readily powdered if desired. Serves 4

Preparation time: 10 minutes   **Cooking time:** 30 minutes

2 tablespoons sunflower oil
1 teaspoon cumin seeds
2 teaspoons ginger-garlic paste
1 fresh green chilli, minced
2 tablespoons tomato purée
1 teaspoon turmeric powder
2 large potatoes, peeled and cubed
150g (5oz) green peas, shelled if fresh, or frozen
Salt

1 Heat the sunflower oil in a wok or shallow saucepan.

2 Add the cumin seeds and allow them to darken. This happens quite quickly so make sure that your next ingredient is to hand.

3 Mix in the ginger-garlic paste and the green chilli.

4 Stir in the tomato purée and the turmeric powder. Add a few tablespoons of water so that the spices cook and the oil separates.

5 Add the potatoes and fresh peas, if using, and season with salt. If using frozen peas, add them when the potatoes are half cooked.

6 Pour in 300ml (10fl oz) hot water and bring to the boil. Reduce the heat, cover and cook until the vegetables are done. You may need to add more water if the curry dries up.

7 Serve hot, with a sprinkling of fresh coriander, if desired.

Dum Aloo

Kashmir, the beautiful Himalayan state in northern India is known for its frugal but distinctive cuisine that is rich in spiced meats, nuts and dried fruit. This is one of India's most popular dishes, and is served in restaurants all over the country. There are many recipes for it, some richer than others. This one is an updated, modern version. 'Dum' means cooking in steam and is a popular style in north India. Serves 4

Preparation time: 10 minutes   **Cooking time:** 45 minutes

300g (10oz) small new potatoes
Sunflower oil for deep frying
3 tablespoons tomato purée
1 teaspoon powdered fennel
1 teaspoon powdered ginger
1/2 teaspoon dried mint leaves, crumbled to a powder
Salt
150ml (5fl oz) single cream

1 Prick the potatoes with a fork and reserve. Heat the oil in a deep, heavy-bottomed saucepan. Fry the potatoes in batches until crisp and golden. (They do not need to be completely cooked at this stage.)

2 Remove the potatoes with a slotted spoon and drain on kitchen paper.

3 Put 2 tablespoons of the hot oil in another saucepan and add the tomato purée. Cook until the oil separates, stirring frequently to prevent it from sticking.

4 Add the spice powders and the mint, reserving a pinch for the garnish. Season with salt. Pour in about 50ml (2fl oz) hot water, cover tightly and cook on a low heat until done. The steam in the pan will cook the potatoes in about 5–7 minutes.

5 Pour in the cream and heat through. Serve warm, dusted with the reserved dried mint powder.

Gajar Kobi nu Shak   Makkai Tamater

Gujarati cooking is delicate, mostly vegetarian, and noted for unusual ingredients and combinations. Vegetables are not smothered in spices; instead they are lightly cooked with a few flavourings to bring out their freshness and unique taste. The Gujarati 'thali', now reserved for special occasions, consists of small bowls of sweet and savoury dishes presented on a large platter and served with poories, rice and a sweet. Serves 4

Preparation time: 10 minutes   **Cooking time:** 25 minutes

2 tablespoons sunflower oil
1 teaspoon black mustard seeds
2 green chillies, slit down the middle
1 teaspoon fresh, grated ginger
1 teaspoon turmeric powder
300g (10oz) cabbage, shredded
300g (10oz) carrots, grated
Salt

1 Heat the oil in a wok or a heavy-bottomed saucepan. Add the mustard seeds and let them pop. Add the chillies and the ginger. Stir for a few seconds. Sprinkle in the turmeric powder and stir.

2 Add the cabbage and the carrots, season with salt and stir until the vegetables start to turn translucent. Pour in about 150ml (5fl oz) hot water. Cover the pan and cook on low heat, adding a little water as necessary, until the vegetables are done but still have 'bite'.

3 Serve hot. This dish is traditionally served sprinkled with freshly grated coconut.

Sweetcorn grows all over India and is eaten in a variety of ways: on the cob, as kernels, and as flour to make bread. Sweetcorn, fresh or tinned, absorbs flavours beautifully and in this recipe it pulls in the tang of tomatoes to create a dish full of juicy flavour and texture. Serves 4

Preparation time: 10 minutes   **Cooking time:** 20 minutes

2 tablespoons sunflower oil
1 teaspoon cumin seeds
1 teaspoon turmeric powder
2 green chillies, finely chopped
3 large juicy tomatoes, chopped
300g (10oz) sweetcorn kernels, cooked
Salt
Few fresh coriander stalks, leaves finely chopped, stems discarded

1 Heat the oil in a heavy-bottomed saucepan and fry the cumin seeds for a few seconds until they start to darken. Sprinkle in the turmeric powder and add the green chillies.

2 Stir in the tomatoes and cook until they soften but remain a bit chunky.

3 Add the sweetcorn and season with salt.

5 Pour in 300ml (10fl oz) hot water and bring to the boil. Reduce the heat and simmer for a few minutes so that the kernels absorb the spice flavours and the oil starts to separate (usually a sign that the spices are cooked).

6 Serve hot with rotis or rice and with the coriander sprinkled on top.

OKRA IN DELICATE YOGURT CURRY

Bhindi Kadhi

Yogurt curry is called kadhi and is made in every corner of India, in many forms. In the north, it is flavoured with little flour dumplings called pakode; in Gujarat in the west, with an assortment of vegetables such as okra; and in the south with spices. It is always eaten with rice and goes well with a crunchy poppadum. Gram flour is used to make onion bhajis and pakoras. It is available in all Indian grocery shops. Serves 4

Preparation time: 10 minutes **Cooking time:** 35 minutes

150g (5fl oz) natural yogurt
2 tablespoons gram flour
2 tablespoons sunflower oil
1 teaspoon black mustard seeds
1 teaspoon turmeric powder
1/2 teaspoon fresh ginger, grated
150g (5oz) okra, tops cut off and each one halved lengthways
Salt

1 Combine the yogurt and the gram flour in a large bowl. Slowly add enough cold water, whisking all the while to remove any lumps, to make a soupy consistency. Reserve.

2 Heat the oil in a heavy-bottomed saucepan and add the mustard seeds. As they begin to pop, add the turmeric powder and the ginger, reserving some of it to garnish.

3 Add the okra, season with salt and stir gently until the okra is coated with the spices.

4 Cover the pan with a concave lid designed to hold water. Fill the lid with cold water. (As the vapours in the pan rise and hit the cold lid above, they condense back into the pan to cook the okra.)

5 After about 10 minutes, pour in the yogurt and flour mixture. When it is quite hot but not boiling, reduce the heat and cook on a low heat until the sauce thickens.

6 Keep stirring to prevent it from curdling. If this should happen, whisk the curry lightly. Taste the curry to check that it has lost the raw flour flavour.

7 Serve hot, sprinkled with the ginger.

Gucchi Makanwala

Mushrooms are a relatively new ingredient in the Indian kitchen but they have become extremely popular and are now available in every fresh vegetable market. In India, only the white, closed cup variety is available. The curry butter is a new way of presenting an old concept. Traditionally, spices have been fried in ghee or butter to release their flavour; this can result in a greasy dish. I have kept the curry butter separate so that each person can choose how much fat they wish to eat. Serves 4

Preparation time: 10 minutes   **Cooking time:** 25 minutes

3 tablespoons ghee or butter
1/2 teaspoon ginger-garlic paste
300g (10oz) mushrooms, wiped with moistened kitchen paper
1 teaspoon garam masala powder
1 tablespoon lemon juice
Fresh coriander sprigs
Salt

1 Heat 1 tablespoon of ghee or butter in a shallow saucepan and fry the ginger-garlic paste for a few seconds.

2 Add the mushrooms and sauté until slightly browned. Remove from the heat and set aside.

3 Heat the remaining ghee or butter in a separate pan and add the garam masala powder. Fry for just a few seconds and add the lemon juice.

4 Sprinkle in the coriander and season with salt.

5 Remove from the heat, cool and refrigerate until firm.

6 Just before you are ready to serve, remove the butter from the fridge and bring it to room temperature. Re-heat the mushrooms and serve the curry butter separately on the side.

Mattar Yakhni

Yakhni is way of preparing meat or vegetables in a yogurt sauce. The resulting dish is slightly tangy and quite velvety. Here, the smooth flavour of the peas is complemented by the delicacy of the saffron. In India, Kashmir is the source of quality saffron. In the West, you can use Spanish saffron since it is readily available and is exactly the same as the Kashmiri one in colour and flavour. If you want to make this dish in advance, prepare it to step 4 and stir in the yogurt at the last minute. Take the yogurt out of the refrigerator well in advance, otherwise it will cool down the entire dish. Serves 4

Preparation time: 10 minutes   **Cooking time:** 25 minutes

2 tablespoons sunflower oil
1 teaspoon powdered ginger
1 teaspoon powdered fennel seeds
1 teaspoon garam masala powder
300g (10oz) green peas, shelled if fresh, or frozen
Salt
Large pinch saffron
150ml (5fl oz) natural yogurt

1 Heat the oil in a wok or a heavy-bottomed saucepan and tip in the spice powders.

2 Immediately add in the peas and season with salt. Mix well so that the spices do not burn.

3 Pour in 150ml (5fl oz) hot water and bring to the boil.

4 Reduce the heat and add the saffron. If you are using fresh peas, cook them until they are done. If using frozen peas, cook for a few minutes until soft.

5 Whisk the yogurt lightly. Take the peas off the heat and stir in the yogurt.

6 Serve immediately as an accompaniment to a chicken dish, such as Chicken with Tomato and Fresh Coriander (page 74).

Pyaz aur Paneer ki Bhurji

Every Indian home has a store of onions and potatoes. At times, the onion supply may be of several different varieties – red, pink, purple or white. These are considered cooling and healthy during the hot months. My grandmother would seasonally buy her stock of white pearl onions that were sold on straw ropes, just as garlic is sold in the West. Even today, my kitchen in India has a special hook on which I hang my own rope of onions every year. *Serves 4*

Preparation time: 15 minutes **Cooking time:** 15 minutes

2 tablespoons sunflower oil
1 teaspoon cumin seeds
1 bunch spring onions, green and white parts chopped
2 red onions, sliced finely
2 green chillies, slit down the middle
Salt
2 tablespoons fresh coriander leaves, chopped
150g (5oz) paneer, grated into large shreds

1 Heat the oil in a wok or a shallow saucepan.

2 Add the cumin seeds and allow to darken. Tip in the spring and red onions and stir fry until soft.

3 Stir in the chillies and season with salt. Sprinkle in the coriander leaves.

4 Serve hot, garnished liberally with the grated paneer.

5 Serve as an accompaniment to rice and lentils, such as Sweet and Sour Lentils (page 106).

Hyderabadi Baingan

This is another classic dish from the former royal state of Hyderabad, situated in the central south of India. It is quite a richly flavoured dish and goes well with plain rice or rotis. I serve it with nothing but a crunchy green salad. I first made this dish when I was a teenager and it was such a hit that I was regularly called upon by my family to make it when we were entertaining. Serves 4

Preparation time: 10 minutes **Cooking time:** 45 minutes

Sunflower oil for deep frying
1 large aubergine, cubed
1 teaspoon turmeric powder
1 teaspoon chilli powder
2 tablespoons tamarind pulp
2 tablespoons soft brown sugar
6 fresh curry leaves
Salt

1 Heat the oil in a deep, heavy-bottomed saucepan. When it is almost smoking, fry the aubergine quickly, until it is golden in colour. It is important to have the oil really hot, or else the aubergine will need to remain in the oil longer and will needlessly absorb more oil.

2 Put 2 tablespoons of the hot oil in another saucepan and add the spice powders. Almost immediately, add the tamarind, sugar and curry leaves.

3 Cook for a couple of minutes until you get a thick sauce.

4 Add the fried aubergine, season with salt and cook for a few minutes, mixing gently to blend into the sauce. Serve hot.

An everyday home-cooked meal in India comprises roti or bread, rice, dal or some kind of lentils, a vegetable dish and a salad. Lentils form the protein component of the vegetarian meal. They are cooked in every part of the country in a variety of recipes. In the north, they are flavoured with onions and cumin whereas in the south, they are made into sambhar, seasoned with a multitude of spices.

In India, a meal is composed keeping in mind the season, geography, social and religious customs and even medical beliefs. For example, in the heat of the Rajasthani desert, lentils will be flavoured with sizzling-hot red chillies that are likely to make the consumer break out in a sweat! This actually helps to bring down the body temperature keeping the body cool.

Lentils are highly prized in Ayurveda, the ancient Indian system of holistic healing. They are combined with rice and a few flavourings to make a variety of khichadis which are creamy preparations not unlike the kedgeree available in the West. Khichadis are easy to digest, quite energising and are used extensively in panchkarma, an ayurvedic cleansing therapy.

Many kinds of lentils are used in Indian cooking. Among the most popular are yellow lentils called toor or arhar dal. These are most popular in Gujarat and the south. Much prized in the north is the black lentil or urad dal which is quite creamy and is often combined with red kidney beans to make a classic dish called Kali Dal.

Indians use lentils in three main ways: cooked whole, as with green mung beans or whole red lentils which are actually brown in colour; split into two halves with the skins on; and lastly, split, without the skin. Each variety has a unique flavour and texture.

Among the beans, butter beans, chickpeas, dried black-eyed beans, brown chickpeas and red kidney beans are the main choices. These are most often sold in their dried form or these days you can buy them ready-cooked in cans. They are eaten with rice or bread and can be made into salads, stews or soups. They are always served as a part of the Gujarati thali – literally, a big metal plate with tiny bowls containing a variety of vegetarian dishes. There is a proper way to serve food in a thali with the dry dishes to the left, the more liquid ones to the right. Various kinds of beans are made into sweet and sour preparations that go with tiny poories.

Lentils & Beans

Masoor Masala

Palak ki Dal

Red lentils are popular with the Parsees, as well as the Maharashtrians who live in and around Mumbai. Whole red lentils are brown in colour with a musky, chewy taste. They are often seen in their split form as red lentils. Soaking whole lentils overnight helps reduce cooking time. Serves 4

This is a real favourite in my home: both delicious and healthy. The creaminess of the spinach blends beautifully with the grainy lentils. Serve with plain boiled rice and a vegetable such as Hyderabad-style Sweet and Sour Aubergines (page 100). Serves 4

Preparation time: 10 minutes + soaking **Cooking time:** 45 minutes

Preparation time: 10 minutes **Cooking time:** 30 minutes

300g (10oz) whole red lentils or masoor, covered and soaked
  overnight in water
2 tablespoons sunflower oil
1 large onion, finely sliced
2 teaspoons ginger-garlic paste
2 fresh tomatoes, finely chopped
1 teaspoon turmeric powder
1 teaspoon chilli powder
Salt
2 tablespoons coriander leaves, freshly chopped

150g (5oz) split red lentils, washed and drained
150g (5oz) spinach, washed thoroughly and cut into strips
2 tablespoons sunflower oil
2 garlic cloves, kept whole and lightly crushed
1 teaspoon turmeric powder
1 teaspoon chilli powder
2 teaspoons lemon juice
Salt

1 Drain the soaked lentils and cover with about 600ml (1¼ pints) hot water. Bring to the boil then reduce the heat and cook until mushy.

2 Heat the oil in a heavy-bottomed saucepan and fry the onion until golden. Remove half with a slotted spoon and reserve. Season lightly.

3 Add the ginger-garlic paste to the pan and stir for a few seconds.

4 Tip in the tomatoes and the spice powders and cook until soft. Season with salt and stir in the cooked lentils.

5 Serve hot, topped with the reserved fried onion and coriander leaves.

1 Cover the lentils with about 300ml (10fl oz) hot water. Bring to the boil then reduce the heat and simmer until mushy. You may need to add more water if the lentils dry out. When done, they will have turned yellow.

2 Meanwhile, boil a little water in another pan and sweat the spinach for a few minutes. (Keep the pan uncovered to keep its colour.) Reserve.

3 Heat the oil in a wok or heavy-bottomed saucepan and fry the garlic until golden. Sprinkle in the spice powders.

4 Pour in the cooked lentils at once. Add the spinach along with its cooking water to the pan. Mix well.

5 Add the lemon juice and season with salt. Heat through and serve hot.

Khatti Meethi Dal

Pind di Da

This recipe is traditionally made with jaggery, a sweet-tasting by-product of the manufacture of sugar from sugar cane. It is unrefined and therefore quite sticky and crumbly. When heated, it melts down to a gooey paste and has a heavy caramel-like aroma that has been described as slightly alcoholic. The musky flavour adds a whole new dimension to many sweets and to some lentils. It also goes well with tamarind. If you cannot find jaggery, soft brown sugar makes an acceptable substitute. Serves 4

Preparation time: 10 minutes   **Cooking time:** 45 minutes

150g (5oz) split red lentils, washed and drained
2 tablespoons sunflower oil
1 teaspoon black mustard seeds
1 teaspoon turmeric powder
2 tablespoons tamarind pulp
1½ tablespoons jaggery or soft brown sugar
2 tablespoons roasted peanuts
Salt

1 Cover the lentils with about 300ml (10fl oz) hot water. Bring to the boil then reduce the heat and cook until they are mushy. Remove from the heat and reserve.

2 Heat the oil in a saucepan and fry the mustard seeds until they pop.

3 Reduce the heat and add the turmeric powder, stir and add the tamarind and the jaggery or sugar. Stir until well blended.

4 Pour in the lentils, add the peanuts and season with salt. Heat through until almost boiling and serve hot with boiled rice.

In Punjab the winters are rough and relentless, the summers scorching. Punjabis therefore use lot of ghee (clarified butter) in their cooking. Ghee acts as a lubricant in the cold, keeping the digestion as well as the skin well toned. In summer, it is cooling and helps to balance the heat within the body. Ghee is available in Indian grocery shops but you can make it easily: melt unsalted butter and skim off the foam that rises to the top. When the melted butter becomes clear and golden, the ghee is ready. Discard any residue at the bottom of the pan. Serves 4

Preparation time: 15 minutes **Cooking time:** 35 minutes

150g (5oz) yellow lentils or toor dal
1 large onion, finely chopped
2 fresh green chillies, finely chopped
2 teaspoons ginger-garlic paste
2 tablespoons tomato purée
1 teaspoon turmeric powder
Salt
2 tablespoons ghee

1 Put the lentils, onion, green chillies, ginger-garlic paste, tomato purée and turmeric powder in a heavy-bottomed saucepan and pour in about 300ml (10fl oz) hot water.

2 Bring to the boil, reduce the heat and cook until the lentils are very soft and mushy. By this time, the onion will have almost melted into the dal.

3 Season with salt and add the ghee. Serve hot with a roti or with rice and some ready-made lime pickle. Heaven!

Jeeryachi Amti

Cumin can sometimes be confused with caraway seeds as both look so similar. Cumin is longer and has fine ridges along each seed. In India it is prized for its medicinal properties which include helping the digestion and calming a cold. Unlike some spices such as black cardamom, which features far more in northern cookery, cumin is widely used in India's regional cookery and as such is available everywhere. Serves 4

Preparation time: 10 minutes   **Cooking time:** 40 minutes

150g (5oz) split mung beans, washed and drained
2 tablespoons sunflower oil
1 teaspoon cumin seeds
1 red onion, finely sliced
1 teaspoon ginger-garlic paste
1 teaspoon turmeric powder
2 teaspoons lemon juice
Salt
1 tablespoon fresh coriander leaves, chopped

1 Cover the beans with about 300ml (10fl oz) hot water. Bring to the boil then reduce the heat and cook until mushy. You may need to add more water if the beans dry out. When they are done, they will have turned yellow.

2 Heat the oil in another pan and fry the cumin seeds for a few seconds until they darken.

3 Add the onion and fry until soft. Stir in the ginger-garlic paste.

4 Sprinkle in the turmeric powder and stir for a few seconds.

5 Pour in the cooked beans, add the lemon juice and season with salt.

6 Heat through and serve hot, garnished with the fresh coriander leaves.

This goes well with rice and a spicy chicken dish such as Tandoori-style Baked Red Chicken (page 78).

Dosa

This is a fabulous dish from south India and one that is served at any time of the day. My family is part south Indian and I have enjoyed dosas for breakfast, as a teatime snack and for dinner. They are served with a variety of chutneys made with coconut, tangy raw mangoes, red chillies or curry leaves. They can also be filled with a spicy potato mix, called masala dosas, or served with a lovely meat or chicken curry.

Please don't be put off by the long preparation time. The final dish is worth it and all it needs is a little advance planning! Serves 4

Preparation time: 15 minutes + soaking + 2 hours fermenting
Cooking time: 25 minutes

300g (10oz) basmati rice or broken basmati rice, washed and drained
150g (5oz) split skinless black lentils, washed and drained
Salt
6 tablespoons sunflower oil for frying

1 Soak the rice and the lentils separately in plenty of water, preferably overnight or for at least 4 hours.

2 Drain away the water and grind them separately in a blender, adding a little water as necessary, until you get two smooth, thick batters. Combine these batters and season with salt. Leave to ferment in a warm place for a couple of hours.

3 Heat a flat-based iron griddle or a nonstick pan and pour in 1 teaspoon oil.

4 Stir the batter well and pour a ladleful of it into the centre of the pan. Spread the mixture quickly making a neat, small circle.

5 Drizzle a few drops of oil around the edges of the pancake. Reduce the heat, cover the pan and cook for a few seconds. Turn the pancake over with a spatula and cook the other side. (You may have to discard the first pancake if it is sticky and irregular in shape. Not to worry: the first one seems to season the pan for those that follow.)

6 Continue similarly with the rest of the batter, keeping the pancakes warm as you go, and serve immediately.

Chavli khumb

I mostly use dried beans as they are cheaper, take up less space to store and seem more flavourful. However, canned cooked black-eyed beans are available and are quite acceptable. Here I have combined them with mushrooms, making this a stunning and elegant dish for a vegetarian meal. Serve it with Goan Sausage and Herb Salad (page 118) for a summer feast. Serves 4

Preparation time: 10 minutes **Cooking time:** 45 minutes

150g (5oz) dried black-eyed beans, covered and soaked overnight in water
3 tablespoons sunflower oil
1 teaspoon cumin seeds
1 large onion, finely sliced
1 teaspoon ginger-garlic paste
1½ teaspoons turmeric powder
1½ teaspoons chilli powder
Salt
300g (10oz) closed cup mushrooms, wiped with moistened kitchen paper

1 Drain off the water in which the beans have been soaked. Cover the beans with about 300ml (10fl oz) fresh hot water. Bring to the boil then cook until they are well done but still hold their shape. Remove from the heat and reserve.

2 Meanwhile, heat the oil in a heavy-bottomed saucepan and fry the cumin seeds until they darken.

3 Add the chopped onion and cook until it softens. Mix in the ginger-garlic paste.

4 Add the spice powders. Season with salt.

5 Divide this mixture into two and pour one half into the hot cooked beans.

6 To the other half, add the mushrooms and stir over a low heat until the mushrooms have softened.

7 To serve, spoon the mushrooms on top of the spiced beans and garnish with a wedge of lemon if desired.

CHICKPEAS WITH COCONUT

Chanya Upkari

CHICKPEAS AND SAUSAGE STEW

Channe ka Shorba

In the past, making a dish with chickpeas meant overnight soaking and endless boiling to ensure that they were cooked through. Today, canned cooked chickpeas are easily available so that dinner can be on the table in a matter of minutes. I have always said that with a few spices, a can of chickpeas and a handful of rice, you can make one of the fastest Indian meals possible! Serves 4

Preparation time: 10 minutes **Cooking time:** 15 minutes

2 tablespoons sunflower oil
1 teaspoon black mustard seeds
5 fresh curry leaves
2 red chillies, stalks pinched off, seeds shaken out
1x 400g (14oz) can chickpeas, drained
2 tablespoons desiccated coconut
Salt
2 tablespoons fresh coriander leaves, chopped

1 Heat the oil in a wok or heavy-bottomed saucepan and fry the mustard seeds for a few seconds until they pop.

2 Add the curry leaves and the red chillies and stir for about 1 minute.

3 Stir in the chickpeas and the coconut. Season with salt.

4 Heat through and mix in the coriander leaves just before serving.

This dish, inspired by the broths served in north India, can be served as a summer lunch or as a soup before dinner. Chickpeas are very versatile: try them mashed with garlic, onion and lemon juice to make a delightful chutney or tossed over boiled rice for a festive touch. Serves 4

Preparation time: 10 minutes **Cooking time:** 20 minutes

1 tablespoon sunflower oil
1/2 teaspoon cumin seeds
1 teaspoon ginger-garlic paste
6 tablespoons tinned, chopped plum tomatoes
1 x 400g (14 oz) can chickpeas, drained
Salt
2 tablespoons fresh coriander leaves
50g (2oz) paneer or Indian cottage cheese
50g (2oz) chourico (Goan sausage) or chorizo

1 Heat the oil in a heavy-bottomed saucepan and fry the cumin seeds for a few seconds until they darken. Add the ginger-garlic paste and stir for 1 minute or so.

2 Tip in the tomatoes and the chickpeas. Season with salt and pour in 600ml (1 1/4 pints) hot water. Bring to the boil and simmer for a few minutes to blend the flavours.

3 If serving the stew immediately, remove from the heat, stir in the coriander leaves, paneer and chourico. Otherwise, prepare up to step 2 and add the last 3 ingredients just before serving. The paneer and the sausage will soften in the heat of the broth.

Rajma Tikki

This is a variation of a dish that used to be served at my school in Bombay, the old name for Mumbai. Each day, the school canteen would have a different menu and when these patties were on offer, all of us would wait for the break to rush over and buy some before they were sold out. The school ones were made of potatoes but I like to add beans for extra flavour and nutrition. Serves 4

Preparation time: 15 minutes **Cooking time:** 35 minutes

1 x 400g (14oz) can red kidney beans, drained
1 large potato, peeled, boiled and mashed
2 slices white bread, crusts removed
Salt

for the chutney
1 bunch fresh coriander, washed
1 tablespoon ginger-garlic paste
2 green chillies, finely chopped
3 tablespoons desiccated coconut
Salt

Sunflower oil for shallow frying

1 Mash together the beans, the potato and the bread to form a dough. Season with salt and set aside covered with a damp cloth.

2 To make the chutney, put the coriander leaves and tender stems along with the ginger-garlic paste, chillies and coconut in a blender to whizz to a fine paste. Season with salt.

3 Divide the bean dough into 8 equal-sized balls and flatten. Put a little chutney at the centre of each disc and fold the edges over to seal in the chutney. Smooth the surface of the patties.

4 Heat enough oil in a saucepan to shallow fry the patties. When the oil is nearly smoking, place the patties in it. Turn over when one side is golden and cook the other side. Serve hot, with tomato ketchup.

A fresh, crisp salad served with an Indian meal can often be the finishing touch required to make it balanced and complete. With the various spices and sauces used to flavour the dishes, the palate needs a cool, neutral flavour to provide contrast.

Indian salads are often dressed with yogurt which is what defines a raita. Traditional salad dressings also include honey, lemon juice, vinegar, ginger juice and fresh tomato juice. Vegetarian salads are popular and a host of fresh vegetables and fruit, including beetroot, pearl onions, ridge gourds, mangoes, jackfruit and wild berries, join forces to make up an unusual selection of salads.

In a country that thrives on eating fresh ingredients, even the most humble Indian eatery will serve a plate of salad consisting of a few slices of onion, a couple of sticks of cucumber and a slice or two of tomato with the meal. Raw onions seem to complement spicy curries and are often served sliced with a squeeze of lemon on top. Fresh tomatoes are grown in plenty and are cheap. Cooling cucumbers sprinkled with salt are sold throughout the summer on little carts.

Non-vegetarian salads that include meat, fish and eggs are also part of the meal in some parts of India. Anglo-Indian, as well as Parsee, cooking uses mayonnaise as a salad dressing and fish mayonnaise is a popular salad in many restaurants.

Salads & Raitas

MONSOON SALAD

Barkha Bahar

The monsoon season in India is a combination of cool breezes and steaming hot intervals. Most people find that they need a healing palate of food to cope with the changing weather. Ginger is considered to have healing properties and keeps colds and fevers at bay. Select ginger that is really tender and fresh so that you can extract its juice: look for roots with a papery, light-coloured skin rather than a leathery, dark skin. Serves 4

Preparation time: 10 minutes   **Cooking time:** 35 minutes

1 large, ripe mango, peeled, stoned and diced into 1cm (^{1}/2in) pieces
4 thick rings fresh pineapple, cut into 1cm (^{1}/2in) pieces (or use drained, canned rings)
2 bananas
Salt
1 tablespoon fresh lemon juice
5cm (2in) piece very fresh ginger
1 tablespoon soft brown sugar

1 Combine the mango, pineapple and banana in a mixing bowl. (Peel and slice the bananas just before you are ready to begin mixing as they will discolour if left unpeeled for any length of time.)

2 Season with salt and add the lemon juice.

3 Grate the ginger finely and squeeze to collect the juice.

4 Add the ginger juice to the bowl. Sprinkle in the sugar and mix lightly. Serve immediately.

WILD MANGO AND MUSTARD SEED SALAD

Ambya Kuval

This is my grandmother's recipe and a childhood favourite of mine. Although it sounds spicy with the mustard seed and red chillies, it is not. Instead, it is wonderfully juicy and a blend of sweet and tangy tastes. I remember asking for this salad to be made almost every day in the summer, which is the mango season in India. I would then eat it with everything from plain boiled rice to a fried chicken drumstick! Serves 4

Preparation time: 20 minutes   **Cooking time:** 15 minutes

8 small ripe mangoes or 2 large ones
2 tablespoons brown sugar
Salt
1 tablespoon sunflower oil
^{1}/2 teaspoon black mustard seeds
6 curry leaves
2 dried red chillies, stalks pinched off, seeds shaken out

1 Peel the mangoes and keep them whole if small (peach sized). Lightly squeeze them to soften. If the mangoes are larger, remove the stones and cube the flesh. Place them in a saucepan with 300ml (10fl oz) water, sugar and some salt and bring to the boil. Reduce the heat and simmer until the mangoes are cooked and the mixture is semi-dry, for about 10 minutes.

2 Heat the oil in a wok or small saucepan and fry the mustard seeds until they pop.

3 Reduce the heat and add the curry leaves and the chillies.

4 Pour this oil with the spices into the mangoes. Mix lightly. Let the salad cool and serve at room temperature.

GOAN SAUSAGE AND HERB SALAD

Goenchi Koshimbir

SPROUTED MUNG BEAN SALAD

Misal

Goans eat pork in many forms – as sausages, ham and fresh in curries and stews. Chourico is a sharp-tasting sausage which is combined in this recipe with an infused oil. Flavoured oils are quite traditional in Indian cookery. To make this oil the first step, as in almost all savoury recipes, is to fry the lemon and herb in the hot oil. Serves 4

Preparation time: 20 minutes **Cooking time:** 15 minutes

150g (5oz) chourico (Goan sausage) or chorizo
1 large tomato, sliced
1 red onion, sliced
2 tablespoons lemon- and herb-infused olive oil
Salt
Pinch of sugar
2 tablespoons fresh coriander leaves, chopped

1 Combine the sausage, tomato, onion and oil in a salad bowl.

2 Season with salt, sprinkle in the sugar and serve immediately, garnished with the chopped coriander.

This is a high protein salad from Mumbai and is a popular snack at any time of the day. The process of sprouting induces many biochemical changes where complex substances are broken down into simple components that are easier to digest. Sprouted legumes have higher levels of Vitamin C, iron and calcium than unsprouted ones.

Preparation time: 10 minutes + 6 hours soaking and overnight sprouting **Cooking time:** 10 minutes

150g (5oz) dried whole mung beans
1 small onion, finely chopped
2 tablespoons fresh coriander leaves, washed and finely chopped
Salt
2 fresh green chillies, finely chopped
Sugar
8 tablespoons natural yogurt

1 Rinse the mung beans, then soak them in warm water for at least 6 hours. Drain and tie them in a clean kitchen towel. Keep them in a warm place overnight, so that they start to sprout. I leave mine until the sprouts are about half a centimetre long!

2 Steam the beans in a steamer, for about 10 minutes until they are cooked but firm.

3 Cool the beans and gently fold in the coriander leaves, salt, chillies and a big pinch of sugar. Serve at room temperature and drizzle the yogurt over the beans.

Ananas Pachadi

This salad is served at a Kerala wedding feast. The whole meal is served on a fresh banana leaf which is large enough to replace a plate. The banana leaf is organic, biodegradable, beautiful to look at and easy to dispose of. Traditional wedding feasts all over the south are served in this manner. There is also a set way of arranging the dishes on the leaf. At the end of the meal, guests are offered paan – little triangles of betel leaf stuffed with mouth-freshening spices and jams. Serves 4

Preparation time: 20 minutes   **Cooking time:** 20 minutes

1 small fresh pineapple, or 4 rings canned pineapple
Pinch of salt
1/2 teaspoon turmeric powder
1 tablespoon sunflower oil
1 teaspoon black mustard seeds
4 curry leaves
2 large dried red chillies, stalks pinched off, seeds shaken out
2 tablespoons freshly grated or desiccated coconut

1 Prepare the fresh pineapple by holding it upright and thinly slicing off the skin. Prick out the 'eyes' with the tip of a potato peeler and slice the fruit vertically, leaving the central core which is inedible. Cut the pineapple flesh or canned rings into 2.5cm (1in) cubes.

2 Put the pineapple with the salt, turmeric and about 150ml (5fl oz) water in a heavy-bottomed saucepan. Bring to the boil, reduce the heat and cook until the water has been absorbed or evaporated. Remove from the heat and allow to cool.

3 Heat the oil in a small saucepan and add the mustard seeds. When they pop, add the curry leaves and the red chillies. Pour this tempering into the cooked pineapple.

4 Stir in the coconut and serve at room temperature.

TINY LENTIL FRITTERS IN SWEET YOGURT

Tahir Vade

The fritters in this recipe can be made with a variety of lentils, but I often choose the split yellow mung ones because they are quick to cook and very easy to digest. They are used in healing recipes that are given to people who need to get back their vitality or energy. They are also a great source of protein. In this recipe, they need to be soaked so that they become soft enough to blend into a batter. Serves 4

Preparation time: 20 minutes + 3 hours soaking
Cooking time: 25 minutes

150g (5oz) split yellow lentils, washed and drained
Salt
Sunflower oil for deep frying
300ml (10fl oz) natural yogurt
2 teaspoons white sugar
1 teaspoon black mustard seeds
3 large dried red chillies, stalks pinched off, seeds shaken out

1 Soak the lentils in plenty of water for at least 3 hours. Drain off the water and grind the lentils in a blender with a few tablespoons of fresh water. The result should be a smooth, grain-free paste, the consistency of thick custard. Season with salt and reserve.

2 Heat the oil in a deep saucepan or wok. When it is nearly smoking drop in a tiny ball of the lentil batter. It should quickly rise to the top. Reduce the heat slightly and gently drop a few tablespoons of the batter into the oil. (If the balls break up, you could add a couple of tablespoons of gram flour to the batter.) Turn them around a few times to brown them evenly. Don't hurry them along or they will brown on the outside but remain uncooked in the middle.

3 When done, remove the fritters on a slotted spoon and drain them on kitchen paper. Continue to fry tablespoons of batter similarly.

4 In another bowl, whisk together the yogurt, a little salt and the sugar.

5 Heat a tablespoon of oil in a small saucepan and fry the mustard seeds until they pop. Add the red chillies and pour this tempering along with the oil into the seasoned yogurt.

6 Just before serving, lightly add the fritters to the yogurt. Some cooks dip them in water, squeeze them dry and then add them to the yogurt. This softens them and helps them absorb the yogurt. If you like the fritters crisp, add them directly into the yogurt.

7 Serve cool.

Ande Aur Gosht Ka Salaad

Alyache Raita

The Anglo-Indian community has a cuisine that is an exciting blend of East and West. Many of their dishes seem like westernized versions of Indian ones. Mayonnaise is very popular in Indian cities and most hotels include mayonnaise-based salads in their lunch and dinner buffets. The Parsee community too has many specialities using this cold egg sauce. Serves 4

Preparation time: 10 minutes   **Cooking time:** 45 minutes

5 tablespoons mayonnaise (reduced-calorie if desired)
Salt
1 teaspoon white sugar
1 teaspoon garam masala powder
2 tablespoons fresh coriander leaves, washed, drained and
   finely chopped
4 large eggs, hard boiled, shelled and cut into chunks
150g (5oz) lean lamb, cubed and poached in water

1 Combine the mayonnaise, salt, sugar, garam masala powder and coriander leaves in a glass serving bowl. Mix well.

2 Fold in the egg and the cooked lamb. Adjust the seasoning and serve immediately.

The fragrance of ginger is refreshing and warm. It is a versatile ingredient used both in sweet as well as savoury dishes. Use the freshest ginger for this raita as you need to crush it into a fine paste without any bits. I find that in order to do this, I need to buy fine skinned ginger, grate it to discard the fibrous bits and then whizz it in a small blender with all the other ingredients. Serves 4

Preparation time: 15 minutes

2 tablespoons fresh grated ginger
150ml (5fl oz) natural yogurt
Salt
1½ teaspoons sugar
1 teaspoon raisins
2 tablespoons desiccated or freshly shredded coconut

1 Put the ginger and half the yogurt in a small blender and whizz until very fine.

2 Pour into a small serving bowl and stir in the rest of the yogurt.

3 Season with salt, add the sugar and stir to dissolve.

4 Mix in the raisins and serve with the coconut sprinkled on top.

POTATO AND YOGURT SALAD

Aloo Raita

Some vegetables seem to go rather better than others to make wonderful raitas. My favourites are potato and beetroot. Both produce raitas that are creamy and that go well with most curries. I like my potato raita quite chunky and I try to use potatoes that are waxy rather than floury. I have used the rather unhealthy white sugar here for its appearance as this dish is meant to be snowy white. Serves 4

Preparation time: 15 minutes **Cooking time:** 25 minutes

2 medium waxy potatoes (any baking potatoes will do)
300ml (10fl oz) natural yogurt
Salt
1 teaspoon white sugar
1 teaspoon cumin seeds
2 tablespoons finely chopped coriander leaves

1 Boil the potatoes in water until cooked through. Cool slightly, peel and cut into 1 cm (1/2in) cubes.

2 Meanwhile whisk the yogurt with the salt and sugar. Set aside.

3 Heat a small saucepan and dry roast the cumin seeds until they are brown and crisp. Crush them in a mortar to make a rough powder. Sprinkle this into the yogurt.

4 Gently mix the potato cubes into the yogurt and serve at once, topped with the coriander leaves.

TOMATO, ONION AND CUCUMBER SALAD WITH PEANUTS

Falli Kuchumber

Peanuts are widely used in Gujarati and Maharashtrian cookery and quite especially in festive cooking. They are also sold freshly roasted as a warm snack along the beaches of Mumbai. Fresh peanuts sold in their shells can be seen in Indian markets around the monsoons, during the months of August and September. We poach them in salted water at home, peel them and eat the soft, pink peanuts. Only when dried do peanuts turn hard and brittle. Serves 4

Preparation time: 15 minutes

1 onion, chopped
2 tomatoes, chopped
1/2 cucumber, peeled and chopped
1 teaspoon sunflower oil
Salt
1/2 teaspoon white sugar
2 teaspoons lemon juice
2 tablespoons roasted peanuts (salted if you wish)

1 Combine the onion, tomato and cucumber in a serving dish.

2 In a separate bowl, mix together the oil, salt, sugar and lemon juice (use only a little salt if you are using salted peanuts). Stir to dissolve the salt and sugar and pour this into the salad.

3 Serve immediately, sprinkled with the peanuts.

CHICKPEA AND PEACH SALAD

Himachali Chaat

BANANA AND CUMIN IN YOGURT

Kele ka Raita

Himachal Pradesh in the north of India is fondly called 'apple country'. It is supremely beautiful with cascading waterfalls and forests of pine trees. Its cool climate enables strawberries, peaches and cherries as well as apples to grow in plenty. The cuisine is quite distinctive and strongly flavoured. I have combined the produce of the region to create this unusual salad. If you are going to prepare this salad to serve later, do not add the salt until the last minute or it will make the peaches watery. Serves 4

Preparation time: 20 minutes

1x 400g (14oz) can chickpeas, drained
2 fresh peaches, skinned if liked, stoned and sliced or, if unavailable,
3 tablespoons canned sliced peaches, drained
1/2 teaspoon amchoor (mango powder)
Pinch of garam masala powder
Salt
1 onion, finely sliced
1 tablespoon sunflower oil
1/2 teaspoon fennel seeds

1 Combine the chickpeas and peaches in a mixing bowl.

2 Sprinkle in the spice powders and salt. Add the onion. Mix gently and transfer to a serving bowl.

3 Heat the oil in a small saucepan and fry the fennel seeds for 1 minute until they start to turn brown. Pour the oil along with seeds into the salad. Serve immediately.

I often try to include a fruit-based salad with dinner. Not only does it add a sweetness to complement the spices in the main dishes, but it also gives my family another portion of fruit and vegetables into the daily quota required by everyone for a balanced diet. Choose ripe bananas for this salad as they should be a bit mushy and very sweet. I select the black spotty ones for maximum flavour. Serves 4

Preparation time: 10 minutes

1 teaspoon cumin seeds
300ml (10fl oz) natural yogurt
Salt
2 ripe bananas
1/2 teaspoon red chilli powder

1 Dry roast the cumin seeds in a small saucepan until they darken and smell a bit smoky. Remove from the heat and pound in a mortar or a coffee mill until you get a fine powder.

2 Pour the yogurt into a serving bowl and add the cumin powder, reserving a pinch for the garnish.

3 Season with salt and mix well. Slice the bananas into the yogurt and submerge them so that they do not discolour.

4 Serve at once, sprinkled with the reserved cumin powder and the chilli powder.

Tandoori dishes are almost like barbecued foods because they are made in an open clay oven which is heated with coals at the bottom. There is a great tradition of barbecued foods in India and many cities have small barbecue stalls selling kebabs, goat's liver on skewers, charred chicken nuggets and spiced pieces of seafood.

Although the barbecue as it is understood in the West is not a common feature of Indian life, barbecued food is, and we have a great variety of tikkas and kebabs. Some are marinated in countless spices, others are coated in cheese and butter. Some are skewered and others are made with minced meat shaped like little cakes. Grated raw papaya is often added to the marinade to tenderise the meat and makes it so soft that it melts in the mouth when eaten.

Barbecued foods are almost always accompanied by relishes and salads. Mint chutney is a perennial favourite and a lemon-infused onion salad is a must.

There is a very famous barbecued meat shop in Mumbai behind the Taj Mahal Hotel. The reputation of Bade Miyan is so hot that there are long queues to sample the fare and people travel long distances just to taste the delicious kebabs.

Barbecues

SPICY CHARRED FISH

Mahi Masala

In Mumbai, small beach stalls sell this dish using freshly landed sea fish, such as pomfret or kingfish. Pomfret may not be easily available outside India and if you cannot get hold of kingfish, you could try this with a firm fish such as cod, though you will lose a bit of the sea flavour. Make sure you buy very fresh fish, and it will taste divine, simply served with a few onion rings and a wedge of lemon. Serves 4

Preparation time: 15 minutes + 30 minutes marinating
Cooking time: 25 minutes

5 garlic cloves, finely grated
1 tablespoon coriander seed powder
1 teaspoon cumin seed powder
1 teaspoon red chilli powder
1 teaspoon turmeric powder
Salt
3 tablespoons sunflower oil
4 x firm fish steaks or fillets (such as cod) weighing about 300g (10oz)

1 Combine the garlic with the spice powders in a small mixing bowl. Season with salt. Pour in the oil and mix well to make a paste.

2 Smear this seasoning onto the fish and keep covered for at least 30 minutes.

3 Lift the fish steaks or fillets on a prepared barbecue and cook for about 10–12 minutes on each side until cooked through and slightly charred. Baste with a little oil if you find the fish going dry. Serve immediately.

CORN ON THE COB WITH CHILLI AND LEMON

Bhutta

This is another recipe from my childhood. The beach close to my family home in Mumbai still has a row of carts selling freshly barbecued corn on the cob. The vendor offers you a small bowl containing a mixture of salt and chilli powder and another one containing lemon wedges for you to smear your corn with the desired amount of seasoning. The corn is served in its husk. Perfect for warm evenings as you watch the sun set into the Arabian Sea! Serves 4

Preparation time: 5 minutes **Cooking time:** 15 minutes

4 corn cobs, husks on
1 teaspoon chilli powder
1 teaspoon salt
4 lemon wedges

1 Peel back and yank off the husks of the corn and remove the corn silk. Discard the silk but reserve the husks. Cook the cobs on the barbecue, turning frequently until the grains have popped and blackened.

2 Meanwhile, combine the chilli powder and salt in a small bowl.

3 Serve the hot corn in the reserved husks with the chilli–salt mixture and the wedges of lemon.

4 To eat, dip the lemon wedges in the spice then smear over the corn, squeezing slightly, and repeat the process until you get the desired level of heat and tang.

Samundari Hariyali

Smaller squid are easier to cook than the larger ones which take a very long time. To prepare the squid, cut off the tentacles just in front of the eyes. Pull out the transparent quill and the entrails from the sac and discard. Remove the beak. Pull off any outer membrane from the sac and discard. Wash the sac and tentacles well and pat dry. This dish tastes best when steamed in a banana leaf, but it may be difficult to get one. Instead, use aluminium foil. Serves 4

Preparation time: 20 minutes **Cooking time:** 20 minutes

for the chutney
1 bunch fresh coriander leaves
1 bunch mint leaves
3 green chillies
2 teaspoons ginger-garlic paste
1 teaspoon turmeric powder
Salt
2 tablespoons lemon juice

300g (10oz) small squid, prepared and cut into slices
8 pieces banana leaf (4 to serve the squid on) or aluminium foil

1 To make the green chutney, whizz the coriander and mint leaves, chillies and the ginger-garlic paste in a blender.

2 Mix in the turmeric powder and season with salt. Sprinkle in the lemon juice.

3 Smear this chutney onto the squid slices, divide them into 4 portions and wrap each one in a piece of banana leaf or foil. Secure the parcels with a toothpick.

4 Prepare a steamer and steam the parcels for 15 minutes.

5 Open each parcel and remove the squid slices onto a ready barbecue. Cook for a further 5 minutes until slightly charred.

6 Serve hot on the remaining 4 pieces of banana leaf or foil.

GARLICKY CHICKEN WITH MANGO BUTTER

Tangdi Kabab Ambiya

Chicken with mango may sound unusual but the combination is delightful. In this recipe, which was suggested to me by a dear friend, Mitali, the mango is blended into a smooth butter and served separately. This way, you can choose the level of sweetness you want with your portion of chicken. The butter is a pretty saffron colour and very fragrant.
Serves 4

Preparation time: 15 minutes + 30 minutes marinating
Cooking time: 45 minutes

3 garlic cloves, finely grated
1 teaspoon chilli powder
2 tablespoons lemon juice
Salt
4 chicken legs, skinned and pricked

for the mango butter
1/2 very ripe mango, peeled, stone removed, flesh mashed
4 tablespoons softened butter

1 Combine the garlic, chilli powder, lemon juice and salt in a large mixing bowl. Add the chicken legs and let them stand for at least 30 minutes, overnight if you have the time.

2 Meanwhile, make the mango butter by simply combining the 2 ingredients until you get a fairly smooth consistency. Reserve.

3 When the chicken is well marinated, place it on a hot barbecue and cook on both sides until done and tender right to the bone.

4 Serve at once with the mango butter.

Galavati Kebab

There is an endless variety of kebabs in India and all are suitable for the barbecue. Some are skewered, others are shaped like flat cakes. All are highly flavoured and spiced and are served with an onion salad and wedges of lemon. Kebabs are eaten as starters or are served with drinks as cocktail snacks. More substantial ones are served as a main course with rice or rotis. Serves 4

Preparation time: 10 minutes + 30 minutes marinating
Cooking time: 20 minutes

1 teaspoon chilli powder
1 teaspoon turmeric powder
1 tablespoon garam masala powder
2 teaspoons ginger-garlic paste
Salt
150ml (5fl oz) natural yogurt
300g (10oz) lean lamb, cubed
2 teaspoons rose water

Wooden skewers

1 Combine the spice powders, ginger-garlic paste, salt and yogurt in a large bowl. Mix well.

2 Thread the lamb cubes onto the skewers. Place the skewered meat in the spice mix and allow it to marinate for at least 30 minutes, overnight if you have the time.

3 Cook the lamb along with the marinade on a prepared barbecue, turning them over to cook evenly on all sides. Continue until cooked through and slightly charred, for about 20 minutes.

4 Serve immediately, sprinkled with rose water.

As more and more people discover that not all Indian desserts are extremely sweet and syrupy, they are becoming more appreciated outside of India as well as everywhere within. Each region in India has its own repertoire of sweets. Those from the state of Bengal made with milk and nuts are popular in the form of rasmalai and gulab jamun. Kulfis from north India, flavoured with pistachios and saffron, are available even in major supermarkets in the West.

Throughout the country, given the variety of fresh fruit available all year, many sweets are fruit-based according to their season. In summer, mango fools vie with mango burfies; the red and juicy carrots that fill the winter markets are used for making sweet carrot halwa; and fresh jelly is made with the guavas that are sold in winter from heaped carts.

Milk is readily available and, reduced and thickened, used to make endless burfies and rich puddings. Yogurt is used plain or hung to make curds that form creamy desserts. Cottage cheese or paneer is combined with honey for a fresh finale to the meal. Nuts add crunch and flavour. Spices such as saffron, cardamom and nutmeg add a characteristic zing. Rice pudding, considered food for the gods, is popular everywhere. Often special sweets are made as an offering to the gods and these are distributed as a form of blessing. Every good occasion is celebrated with the distribution of sweets, whether it marks success in exams or the buying of a new house.

In a hot country it is natural that the drinks on offer are varied and many. Most Indians prefer to drink water with their meal in order to appreciate the flavours in the various dishes. Waters flavoured with rose and sandalwood are popular. Lassi, which is simply thinned-down yogurt, is drunk all over India. Flavoured with fruit such as mango or sweetened or salted, it cools the palate beautifully. Fresh fruit juices made with pomegranates, strawberries and oranges are sold at many juice bars. In a country that grows a lot of tea and coffee it is natural that both are popular. They are often flavoured wtih spices such as cardamom and cinnamon. In the summer, tea is infused with fresh ginger or mint leaves.

Puddings & Drinks

CHOCOLATE AND MILK SQUARES

Choclat Burfie

INDIAN ICE CREAM FLAVOURED WITH SAFFRON

Kesar Kulfi

Many people outside of India are unaware that chocolate forms a part of Indian cookery. People often ask me whether chocolate is common in India. In fact it is extremely popular. It is used to flavour many puddings, including some traditional sweets made during the festival of Diwali. No doubt this is a western influence, but chocolate has been and always will be an important food in an Indian home. Makes 20

Preparation time: 5 minutes **Cooking time:** 25 minutes

1 x 400g (14oz) can condensed milk
75g (3oz) butter
110g (4oz) cocoa powder
4 tablespoons mixed chopped nuts

1 Pour the condensed milk into a heavy-bottomed saucepan. Add the butter and cocoa.

2 Cook on a gentle heat, stirring constantly, until the mixture thickens and begins to leave the sides of the pan.

3 Grease a flat dish with the extra butter. Pour in the thick cocoa mixture and smooth the surface with a spatula. Allow to cool and set.

4 Sprinkle with the mixed nuts and cut into 2.5cm (1in) squares. This burfie can be stored in the fridge for up to a week.

Ice cream is a perfect finale to an Indian meal. Its cool creamy sweetness is ideal after a riot of tastes and textures in the main dishes. Kulfi is slightly heavier than western ice creams and is flavoured with fragrant ingredients such as rose, pistachio, cardamom and mango. It is often frozen in little earthen pots – the pot helps to set the kulfi by absorbing some of the moisture. I love to serve kulfi scattered with fresh rose petals. Serves 4

Preparation time: 20 minutes **Cooking time:** 1 hour + freezing

1 teaspoon saffron strands
1.5 litres (2 1/2 pints) full fat milk
300g (10oz) caster sugar
300ml (10fl oz) double cream

1 Soak the saffron in 3 tablespoons of the milk and set aside.

2 Put the remaining milk in a heavy-bottomed saucepan and bring to the boil. Reduce the heat and simmer, stirring frequently to blend in the skin that forms, and to make sure that the milk does not stick to the bottom. Cook until it has been reduced by half; it takes about 50 minutes.

3 Add the saffron and its milk to the pan. Add the sugar. Simmer for 10 more minutes, stirring constantly. Remove from the heat and cool the milk.

4 Pour into a shallow pan and put in the freezer. After about 2 hours, when the milk is very cold, whisk in the cream until the mixture is light and frothy.

5 Pour into deep trays and freeze until solid, preferably overnight. Serve in slices.

Rasmalai

Rasmalai is one of the most famous Indian desserts outside of India. The one you eat in restaurants is probably commercially mass made and you will find that this homemade version is more crumbly and delicate. I hang up the paneer for quite a long time to make sure that it does not crumble up too much during the cooking. I sometimes serve the rasmalai in mango-flavoured milk. Just add some mango purée to the milk before serving. Serves 4

Preparation time: 10 minutes + 1 hour draining
Cooking time: 45 minutes

1.8 litres (3 pints) fresh pasteurised milk
Few drops of lemon juice
150g (5oz) sugar
1/2 teaspoon powdered cardamom seeds
Pinch of saffron
2 teaspoons sliced almonds and pistachios

1 Put 1.2 litres (2 pints) of the milk into a pan and bring to the boil. Add the lemon juice and let the milk curdle. Cool, then put the curdled milk into the centre of a clean piece of muslin and hang it up for about 30 minutes allow the whey to drain off.

2 Meanwhile set 1.8 litres (3 pints) of water to boil in a large shallow saucepan and add a couple of tablespoons of the sugar to it.

3 Take the paneer out of the muslin and knead it lightly for about 1 minute. Shape it into balls the size of a small lime and flatten slightly. You should get about 8 balls.

4 Reduce the heat under the boiling water and slip the balls in gently.

5 Drain and remove after about 10 minutes. The water will go milky and bits will break away from the paneer balls but this is normal. Keep the drained balls flat on a plate. They should be quite spongy.

6 In a separate pan, heat the rest of the milk and sugar. Reduce it until it is quite thick, for about 30 minutes, taking care not to let it burn or spill over. Keep it over a fairly low heat. Add the powdered cardamom and the saffron.

7 Remove from the heat, cool and gently add the paneer balls to the milk. Chill well and serve sprinkled with the sliced nuts.

Vermicelli Payasam

This is an easy and quick pudding to make and can be prepared well in advance. Vermicelli is used in sweet as well as savoury Indian dishes. Indian shops sell roasted as well as plain vermicelli. I like to use the plain one as it has a better appearance and neutral flavour. I prefer it cold but it can also be served warm if you prefer. Serves 4

Preparation time: 10 minutes   **Cooking time:** 25 minutes

1 tablespoon ghee or butter
3 tablespoons mixed nuts, chopped
150g (5oz) vermicelli, broken into short lengths
300ml (10fl oz) milk
150ml (5fl oz) canned evaporated milk
5 tablespoons white sugar

1 Heat the ghee or butter in a heavy-bottomed saucepan and fry 2 tablespoons of the nuts for a few minutes, until golden brown.

2 Add the vermicelli and fry until it begins to turn golden, taking care not to over-brown it.

3 Add both the milks and the sugar. Bring to the boil and reduce the heat, scraping down the sides of the pan to return the creamy residue into the milk.

4 Simmer for 12–15 minutes until the vermicelli is soft.

5 Remove from the heat and pour into individual serving bowls. Sprinkle with the mixed nuts. Allow to cool thoroughly then chill in the refrigerator if serving cold, or you can serve it warm.

Elaichi Custer

The Parsee community in India has a special wedding feast with many meat, chicken and egg preparations that are not a common feature of most Hindu wedding feasts where food is largely vegetarian. A rich version of this recipe is always served at the end of the feast. Traditionally it contains mava which is made by cooking milk until it reduces down to a crumbly cake. I have omitted this to make a lighter pudding which can be served with fresh fruit if desired. I love it on its own. Serves 4

Preparation time: 10 minutes   **Cooking time:** 1 hour 10 minutes

2 pints (1.2 litres) pasteurised milk
90g (scant 4oz) granulated sugar
6 eggs
1 teaspoon vanilla essence
Few good shavings of nutmeg
2 teaspoons sliced almonds

1 Mix the sugar into the milk and set it to boil in a heavy-bottomed saucepan. Allow it to reduce by half, keeping it over a fairly low heat.

2 Remove from the heat and cool completely. Whisk the eggs and fold into the milk.

3 Add the vanilla essence, nutmeg and almonds.

4 Grease a 20cm (8in) soufflé dish and pour in the custard mixture.

5 Place the dish in a bain marie or a tray of water. The water should be at least halfway up the soufflé dish.

6 Bake in a moderate oven at 180°C/350°F/gas 4 for about 45 minutes. The custard should be firm and golden on top but a bit wobbly if shaken. It will continue to set as it cools down outside the oven. A skewer inserted into the middle should come out clean.

7 Chill for a couple of hours before serving.

STEAMED SWEET YOGURT

Bhapa Dhoi

*Yogurt is an essential ingredient in Indian cookery and almost all Indian homes make their own. It is only recently that yogurt has become available in cartons. For large quantities, people go to their local dairy which will sell all milk products including cream, milk that has been cooked and reduced to a solid cake, yogurt and butter. Each dairy produces its own range of products, freshly made each morning.
Serves 4*

Preparation time: 5 minutes + 30 minutes draining time
Cooking time: 20 minutes

150g (5oz) natural set yogurt
1 x 400g (14 oz) can condensed milk
Large pinch powdered cardamom seeds
2 teaspoons chopped mixed nuts and raisins

1 Put the yogurt into the middle of a clean piece of muslin and tie the cloth over the pan to catch the whey. Discard the whey and leave the yogurt for about 30 minutes hanging over a sink to drain off all the whey.

2 Put the drained yogurt into a heatproof mixing bowl and stir in the condensed milk and the powdered cardamom seeds.

3 Cover the bowl with aluminium foil or greaseproof paper. Steam in a steamer or over a large pan of boiling water for 15–20 minutes.

4 Allow to cool, dish into individual serving glasses and serve chilled, sprinkled with the nuts and raisins.

LYCHEES IN ROSE-FLAVOURED COCONUT MILK

Lychee Kheer

When I was growing up in Bombay (as Mumbai was known then) we never thought of lychees as being a particularly Chinese fruit because, at the start of the monsoon season every year, our local fruit market would be filled with bunches of lychees. The fruit would look luscious, pink and rough-skinned with wonderfully scented pale flesh. If you are using fresh lychees for this recipe, be sure to prepare them over a bowl to collect all the juice: it makes a delicious drink. Serves 4

Preparation time: 10 minutes + 30 minutes marinating
Cooking time: 20 minutes

300ml (10fl oz) canned coconut milk
3 tablespoons soft brown sugar
Few drops rose essence or 2 tablespoons rose water
Pinch saffron, soaked in 1 tablespoon of hot water
12 fresh lychees or 12 canned lychees, drained
2 tablespoons flaked almonds

1 Pour the coconut milk into a large mixing bowl and add the sugar. Mix well until all the sugar has dissolved.

2 Sprinkle in the rose essence or rose water and the saffron.

3 If using fresh lychees, snap off the stem and peel off the thick papery skin. Check the top of the fruit for any bugs (!) and slice down the middle. Gently prise the flesh from the central stone which is discarded. Add the lychees to the coconut milk.

4 Spoon the mixture into 4 stemmed serving glasses. Cool in the refrigerator and serve scattered with the flaked almonds.

TROPICAL FRUIT SALAD

Phalon ka Chaat

Jackfruit trees grow tall and strong in many parts of south India. The fruits are very large, each the size of a couple of footballs joined together. They have many seeds clothed with sweet yellow flesh which has a distinctive strong fragrance. Two main varieties of jackfruit grow in India – one with crisp, firm flesh is used raw, the other with mushy fibrous flesh is used in cooking where it is mashed further and cooked to a pulp. Buy canned jackfruit for this recipe as fresh jackfruit is difficult to find outside India and is quite tedious to prepare. *Serves 4*

Preparation time: 20 minutes

1 x 400g (14oz) can jackfruit, drained
1 large, ripe fresh mango
1 x 225g (8oz) can tropical fruit cocktail in juice
300ml (10fl oz) orange juice with bits
single cream, to serve

1 Slice the jackfruit thinly. Peel the mango and cut the flesh off the stone into small chunks.

2 Combine the fruits in a serving bowl. Pour in the fruit cocktail.

3 Add the juice and chill for 1 hour.

4 Serve cold with single cream on the side.

BANANA FRITTERS WITH CARDAMOM BUTTER

Muluk

This dessert is inspired by a dish made during the festival of the elephant-headed god, Ganesh. The fritters are fried in ghee, with cardamom mixed into the batter. I prefer to keep the butter (used in place of ghee) separate and I think the cardamom is more fragrant served this way. *Makes 12*

Preparation time: 15 minutes   **Cooking time:** 20 minutes

2 ripe bananas
Pinch of salt
300g (10oz) ground rice or rice flour
3 tablespoons soft brown sugar
3 tablespoons desiccated coconut
Sunflower oil for deep frying
4 teaspoons butter or ghee
5 green cardamom pods, shelled, and seeds crushed finely

1 Slice the bananas into a bowl and mash them. Sprinkle in the salt. Add the ground rice, brown sugar and coconut. Pour in some water, if required, and knead everything together to make a soft dough.

2 Heat the oil in a deep wok or fryer. When nearly smoking reduce the heat slightly. Tear off portions of dough the size of a small lime, and gently lower them into the oil. Fry until golden brown. (Open one and if it is underdone in the centre, reduce the heat further to cook the rest.) Remove and drain well. Keep them warm while you fry the rest.

3 To make the cardamom butter, melt the butter or ghee in a small saucepan. Remove from the heat and add the crushed cardamom. Serve the warm fritters with the spiced butter on the side for dipping.

ROSE LASSI

Gulabi Lassi

Lassi is a slightly thinned-down version of yogurt, seasoned with spices, salt or flavoured with fruit and flowers. Rose lassi is an ideal summer drink because it is both refreshing and cooling to the system. It can also be served at the end of a meal in place of a heavy pudding. I use rose essence for this recipe but do use rose water if you can find some of excellent quality. The fragrance is of utmost importance here. Serves 4

Preparation time: 10 minutes

600ml (1¼ pints) natural yogurt
300ml (10fl oz) water
Sugar
2 teaspoons rose essence
Pink food colour
Pink rose petals to garnish, optional

1 Blend the yogurt, water, sugar, rose essence and food colour in a blender.

2 Chill until cold in the refrigerator.

3 Pour into individual serving glasses and serve topped with a couple of rose petals on the top of each glass.

MANGO AND NOODLE MEDLEY

Aam Ka Falooda

Falooda is a mixture of layered tastes and textures. It is served cold in tall glasses and makes quite a filling pudding. It is flavoured with various fruits and nuts. It often contains subja seeds which grow on a variety of the basil plant. My recipe is a combination of the various falooda desserts I have eaten at several eateries in Mumbai where the hot weather demands any number of ice-cream and falooda shops. Serves 4

Preparation time: 25 minutes   **Cooking time:** 15 minutes

110g (4oz) thick rice noodles, broken into short lengths
1 large, ripe mango
600ml (1¼ pints) milk
5 teaspoons white sugar
4 scoops mango ice cream

1 Boil the noodles in water until very soft. Drain in a colander and refresh under cold water. Reserve.

2 Meanwhile, peel the mango and chop into small bits. Discard the stone.

3 Mix the milk and sugar until all the sugar has dissolved.

4 Layer the mango and cooked rice noodles in 4 tall serving glasses.

5 Pour in the sweetened milk and float a scoop of mango ice cream on top of each glass. Serve immediately. If preparing in advance, add the ice cream just before serving.

SPICY TOMATO JUICE

Tamater Sip

India grows vast quantities of tomatoes and they are very popular in all Indian cookery. They are used in curries and relishes, in drinks and salads. Use the freshest tomatoes for this recipe as it must be quite red, with a sweet aftertaste and also quite nutritious. You could combine this with vodka to make an unusual Bloody Mary. Serves 4

Preparation time: 20 minutes **Cooking time:** 5 minutes

8 large ripe red tomatoes, chopped
Salt
1/2 teaspoon black peppercorns, crushed
2 teaspoons sugar
2 tablespoons fresh lemon juice
1 teaspoon cumin seeds
4 long fresh green chillies, slit down the middle

1 Put the chopped tomatoes in a blender and whizz for 5 minutes. Strain and discard the pulp and seeds. You may need to do this in 2 batches.

2 Season the juice with salt and add the peppercorns and sugar. Stir in the lemon juice and mix well.

3 Heat a small saucepan and dry roast the cumin seeds for 5 minutes until they are dark and brittle. Whizz these in a coffee mill or pound them in a mortar to powder them. Sprinkle them into the juice.

4 Pour the juice into 4 serving glasses and slip a chilli into each one. Top with ice cubes and serve immediately.

GINGER SPICED TEA

Masala Chai

India is largely a tea-drinking nation although many south Indians prefer coffee and we have good coffee plantations in the south. Tea is often flavoured to provide variety or to make it more healing. Spices and herbs are added to the brew for fragrance and flavour. Indian tea is made by boiling tea leaves in water and adding milk to the pan before it is taken off the heat. Indians never add cold milk to their tea as it brings down the temperature of the drink and means in essence that the milk remains 'uncooked'. I have used tea bags in my recipe. Serves 4

Preparation time: 5 minutes **Cooking time:** 15 minutes

4 small pieces fresh ginger, roughly crushed
4 shavings nutmeg
2 cinnamon quills
4 teabags
Milk and sugar to taste

1 Put the kettle on. Put the ginger and spices in a small pan and pour in 4 cups of hot water. Simmer for 10 minutes.

2 Remove from the heat and add the teabags. Allow to stand for 5 minutes.

3 Use a very fine strainer to strain the brew into a teapot and serve with milk and sugar on the side.

CARDAMOM-FLAVOURED COFFEE
Elaichi Kapi

Most south Indian homes serve excellent filter coffee. Indians prefer to make their coffee in milk rather than in water. This means that the resulting drink is rich and creamy and it is usually sweetened with sugar. I love this spiced version and have it after dinner although I do add a bit of hot water to lighten it.   Serves 4

Preparation time: 5 minutes   **Cooking time:** 10 minutes

4 cardamom pods, roughly pounded in a mortar
600ml (1¼ pints) milk
3 teaspoons freshly milled coffee
Sugar to taste

1 Put the cardamom and milk in a milk pan and bring to the boil. Reduce the heat and sprinkle in the coffee grains. Simmer for 5 minutes.

2 Strain into 4 cups and serve at once with sugar on the side.

SUMMER LEMONADE WITH GINGER
Shikanji

In north India, the fiery hot summers demand a store of cooling drinks kept ready in the refrigerator. Visitors to the home are offered this lemonade, made with ginger and saffron. The drink can be as sweet as you like or you could omit the sugar entirely. Try flavouring this lemonade with cardamom in the winter for a more warming drink.   Serves 4

Preparation time: 5 minutes   **Cooking time:** 10 minutes

Juice of 2 lemons
Salt to taste
Sugar to taste
2.5cm (1in) piece very fresh ginger, peeled
Pinch of saffron
Water

1 Put the lemon juice, salt and sugar if using, in a small pan and heat until well blended.

2 Remove from the heat. Put the ginger in a garlic press and squeeze the juice out into the lemon mixture while it is still hot. Grating the ginger first will help speed up this step.

3 Add the saffron. Divide the mixture into 4 tall glasses and top up with cold water. Float some ice cubes on top and serve. The lemon mixture can be stored in the refrigerator for up to 3 days.

Chutneys and relishes are served with every meal whether in a restaurant or in a home. They give a lift to the meal, adding a touch of sweetness, spice or tang depending on the ingredients.

Most homes will have a selection of chutneys and relishes that are kept in the centre of the table so that people may help themselves. They are made in batches that will keep for a week or so. Many use seasonal ingredients so that there is great variety throughout the year. In the hot summers, most chutneys and relishes are made from the many varieties of mangoes available – from the prized Alphonso to the small wild 'ghontamba'. Most homemakers also make pickles for the year and cure them in the sun which is at its hottest during this time.

In the monsoons, ginger comes to the fore. This is a time when many Hindu festivals are celebrated and ginger adds warmth and fragrance to many festive feasts. Winter brings its own ingredients, from the vibrantly coloured turmeric to the delicious and unique mango turmeric, a variety of turmeric that smells of mangoes and is bright saffron in colour. Also very popular at this time is a crisp tangy fruit called 'amla'. Its vitamin C content makes it an invaluable food in the winter and it is cooked to make several kinds of sweet or tangy relishes.

Chutneys & Relishes

HOT TOMATO RELISH

Kasundi

This relish from Gujarat is a combination of tastes: sweet, tangy and hot. I make it in batches during the summer when the ripest, reddest tomatoes can be found. It keeps for about a week in the refrigerator but its versatility means that it is usually finished up quite quickly. I have seen it being eaten as a sandwich spread, on baked potatoes and with barbecued chicken! It can also be added to curries for extra dash. *Serves 4*

Preparation time: 15 minutes **Cooking time:** 20 minutes

2 tablespoons sunflower oil
1/2 teaspoon black mustard seeds
1 teaspoon ginger-garlic paste
3 large, ripe, red tomatoes, chopped
2 fresh green chillies, finely chopped
Salt
1 teaspoon soft brown sugar
2 tablespoons white vinegar

1 Heat the oil in a heavy-bottomed saucepan and fry the mustard seeds for a few minutes until they pop.

2 Add the ginger-garlic paste and fry for 1 minute. Add the tomatoes and the chillies and mix well. Cook for about 12-15 minutes on high heat until the tomatoes are very mushy.

3 Season with salt, stir in the sugar and the vinegar and cook for a couple more minutes to blend.

4 Remove from the heat, cool thoroughly, then store in a clean glass jar in the refrigerator.

KASHMIRI WALNUT CHUTNEY

Akhrot Chutney

This has been inspired by the cooking of Kashmir where walnuts grow in plenty. It is slightly bitter in taste, adding a new dimension to the meal. Kashmiri cooking was influenced by Greek, Roman and Persian invasions many hundred years ago, and passing caravans left their mark too. Poppy seeds, pomegranate, melon seeds and saffron all combine to flavour meat and vegetables. Garam masala is used to spice up curries; yogurt to temper them down. *Serves 4*

Preparation time: 10 minutes

3 tablespoons walnuts
2 teaspoons dried mint leaves, or fresh mint leaves if you prefer
1/2 teaspoon chilli powder
Salt
8 tablespoons natural yogurt

1 Put the walnuts, mint, chilli powder and salt in a small blender. Add half the yogurt. Whizz to a fine paste, adding the rest of the yogurt a spoonful at a time.

2 Serve at room temperature. Any leftover chutney will keep for a couple of days in the refrigerator.

MINT AND TAMARIND CHUTNEY

Pudine Imli ki Chutney

Indians love a bit of spice and tang to pep up their dinner. Seasonal fruits and vegetables are preserved in spices and oils to be enjoyed when no longer in season. Many regional recipes for pickles and relishes exist. This chutney is popular all over India and is often drizzled over yogurt or yogurt-based raitas. You could also add some cooked vegetables, such as potatoes, to a bit of it, to make a tangy salad. Serves 4

Preparation time: 10 minutes **Cooking time:** 20 minutes

50g (2oz) bottled tamarind pulp
50g (2oz) soft brown sugar
50g (2oz) bottled mint sauce
1 teaspoon cumin seeds
1/2 teaspoon chilli powder
Salt

1 Put the tamarind, sugar and mint sauce in a small saucepan and add about 5 tablespoons of water. Bring to the boil, reduce the heat and cook the mixture on low heat for 10 minutes until well blended.

2 Meanwhile, dry roast the cumin seeds for about 5 minutes until they turn dark and brittle. Crush them to a powder in a mortar or a coffee mill.

3 Add the cumin seed powder and the chilli powder to the tamarind mixture and mix well. Season with salt.

4 Serve at room temperature. Store any leftovers for 3–4 days in the refrigerator. This chutney also freezes very well and can be kept frozen for up to a month.

COCONUT AND GARLIC FIREBALL CHUTNEY

Lasne Chitni

A favourite chutney in my household that combines flavour, heat and texture. Its orangey colour is what makes it a fireball, rather than the level of heat. It is easy to make, keeps for a month in the refrigerator and is extremely versatile. My son even has it with chips! I use it in sandwiches, sprinkled over salads and stirred into lentils for extra flavour.   Serves 4

Preparation time: 15 minutes

150g (5oz) desiccated coconut
6 large garlic cloves, peeled
2 tablespoons chilli powder (less if you want a mild chutney)
Salt
1 teaspoon sugar
1 teaspoon mango powder (amchoor)

1 Whizz the desiccated coconut in a blender or coffee mill to reduce it to a coarse powder.

2 Add the rest of the ingredients to the blender or coffee mill and whizz until well blended and grainy.

3 Store in a clean glass jar and serve with everything!

Breads form part of a daily Indian meal. However, in India they are not called breads and each one will have a distinct name. The most popular bread is roti, a flat round disc with a chewy texture. Many kinds of bread are made, ranging from the Punjabi parathas, naans and kulchas to the southern dosas, idlis and appams. These are sometimes flavoured with herbs and spices and only need a bowl of natural yogurt on the side to make a complete meal. Poories, made all over India, are deep fried in oil or ghee and are usually reserved for special occasions. Poories can also be stuffed with spices or flavoured with herbs.

Most breads are made with atta, a wholewheat flour that is slightly browner and coarser than the refined flour used for making cakes and biscuits. The texture of the atta determines the texture of the final bread. A browner atta will result in a coarser textured roti whereas whiter atta will produce soft, fine bread. South Indians often make pancakes with a combination of lentils and rice. These are stuffed with vegetables such as spiced potatoes or flavoured with onions, tomatoes and fresh coriander leaves.

There are innumerable varieties of rice grown all over India, some short grained and sticky, others long grained and fluffy. Some varieties are red in colour while others are pearly white. There is no doubt however, that basmati is the king of Indian rice, fragrant, evenly shaped and milky white. It is now very popular outside India and is considered to be one of the finest rice varieties in the world.

Rice is a versatile ingredient of the Indian store cupboard. It is cooked almost daily in most Indian homes to be eaten with curries and lentils. It is also made into innumerable sweets, flavoured with milk, nuts, spices and coconut. In the south, it is ground into flour to make delicious breakfast pancakes. Rice is also factory pressed to make tiny flakes that are cooked with potatoes or with sugar or jaggery to make pohe, a much-loved snack. Puffed rice which looks like long white translucent popcorn is used in a variety of snacks including the ever-popular Bombay mix of which many versions exist.

I am often asked the secret of cooking perfect rice. Each cook has his or her own recipe but mine is fairly simple and has served me well through many TV shows and cookery demonstrations. Also, it is how I cook rice at home almost every day. See page 7 for my method. It is the final steaming that makes the rice fluffy and separates the grains. To test that rice is completely cooked, taste a few hot grains or see if you can mash them between your thumb and forefinger. Finally, gently run a fork through the cooked rice and serve hot. Rice refrigerates quite well for up to two days in a sealed container. Simply bring it out when required and buzz it in the microwave for a few minutes depending on the wattage of your machine.

Breads & Rice

SPICED BREADCRUMB PANCAKE

Pao Rava Dosa

South Indians are skilled at making pancakes. These are eaten with curries, chutneys or sweet preserves. Some pancake batters must be fermented overnight to make them light and fluffy. This recipe is for instant pancake and I often make it for my kids after school. They eat it with ketchup or fresh tomato relish. Dosas can also be made in advance and re-heated but there is nothing quite like eating them hot off the pan! Serves 4

Preparation time: 10 minutes   **Cooking time:** 25 minutes

300g (10oz) breadcrumbs
2 tablespoons semolina (coarse or fine)
Pinch of turmeric powder
Salt
Sunflower oil to shallow fry

1 Combine the breadcrumbs, semolina, turmeric and salt in a mixing bowl. Pour in enough cold water – about 850ml (1¹/₂ pints) – to make a batter of pouring consistency, almost like thick custard.

2 Heat 1 tablespoon oil in a large saucepan. Pour in a ladleful of the batter into the centre and spread it in quick circles to form a flattish disc about 10cm (4in) in diameter. Cover the pan and allow the pancake to cook in its steam.

3 Flip the pancake over when the underside has turned golden and spotty. Cook the other side by dotting the edges with some oil and covering the pan.

4 Keep the pancakes warm while you make the rest and serve hot. These are served flat as they might crack down the centre if folded.

WATERMELON PANCAKES

Kalingada Pole

This exotic and unusual-sounding dish is actually quite simple to make and is a favourite in my family. Only the white part of the watermelon is used (you see this as a thin section between the red flesh and the green skin). This is because it is bland and slightly crunchy. What a great way to use up what we would normally discard! The pancake tastes slightly sweet and it is served with butter or with a mild vegetable curry. Serves 4

Preparation time: 15 minutes   **Cooking time:** 35 minutes

300g (10oz) coarse semolina
2 tablespoons plain white flour
4 tablespoons of grated watermelon (white part) along with the juice
2 tablespoons soft brown sugar
Salt
Sunflower oil for shallow frying

1 Mix the semolina, flour, watermelon, sugar and salt in a mixing bowl. The water in the watermelon should normally be enough to make a thick batter. If not, add a little extra cold water and stir well.

2 Heat a tablespoonful of oil in a large saucepan. Pour in a ladleful of the batter into the centre and spread it in quick circles to form a flattish disc about 10cm (4in) in diameter. Cover the pan and allow the pancake to cook in its steam.

3 Flip the pancake over when the underside has turned golden. Cook the other side by dotting the edges with some oil and covering the pan.

4 Keep the pancakes warm while you make the rest and serve hot.

FRIED RED BREAD

Lal Poori

Poories are usually made on special occasions such as weddings or at religious or social festivals. They are deep fried and therefore taste quite rich. They go equally well with rich curries as well as milky desserts. In the summer during the Indian mango season, almost every wedding menu in my hometown of Mumbai has aamras-poori on it. This is a classic combination of mango purée and poories. I have added a bit of beetroot to this recipe. It not only gives a delightful pink colour but also helps bring in some extra vegetable content into the meal. Serves 4

Preparation time: 15 minutes **Cooking time:** 30 minutes

450g (1lb) wholewheat flour or atta
1 small cooked beetroot, finely grated
Sunflower oil for deep frying
220ml (scant 1/2 pint) warm water

1 Mix the flour, beetroot and a tablespoon of the oil with your fingers and bind into a stiff dough, adding the warm water a little at a time. You may need more or less water than the quantity given, depending on the quality of the flour.

2 Heat the oil in a deep kadhai or wok. Test the temperature by dropping a tiny ball of dough into the oil. It should float at once.

3 Meanwhile, divide the dough into equal-sized balls the size of large cherries. You should get about 18. Smear your palm with some oil and shape each ball smoothly.

4 Roll out each ball to a flat disc about 2.5cm (1in) in diameter, flouring the board as necessary.

5 Gently lower the disc into the hot oil and press down with the back of a slotted spoon. It will puff up only if the oil is hot enough and the poori is submerged.

6 As soon as it has puffed, turn it over and fry for 1 minute until golden pink.

7 Lift out with a slotted spoon, and drain on kitchen paper.

8 Cook all the poories in the same way. Serve warm.

Roti/Chapati

Limboo Bhath

This is the most commonly made bread in India. It is flaky, bland and a wonderful accompaniment to all the spice and herb flavours in the main dish. The art of making rotis is in getting the dough right and in rolling out perfectly round discs ready to roast. Many young girls in India, as little as seven or eight, start out in the kitchen by helping their mothers to make rotis. My own daughter, who is six, loves to make the balls of dough and roll out what she calls 'maps'. We then eat up whole countries! Serves 4

Preparation time: 10 minutes **Cooking time:** 20 minutes

450g (1lb) wholewheat flour or atta
2 teaspoons sunflower oil
Warm water as needed
Ghee if desired

1 Combine the flour and oil in a bowl. Mix into a pliable dough with warm water. Knead for 5 minutes (the more you knead, the softer the rotis).

2 Divide the dough into portions the size of a lime. Coat lightly with flour, shape into a ball in your palm and flatten slightly.

3 Roll out into flat discs about 10cm (4in) in diameter, flouring the board as necessary.

4 Heat a griddle or shallow pan. Roast the discs on the griddle until the surface appears bubbly. Turn over and press the edges down with a clean cloth to cook evenly. As soon as brown spots appear the roti is done.

5 Remove and smear with ghee. Keep warm by wrapping in foil as you cook all the rotis in the same way. Serve warm.

Rice is prepared in every south Indian household every single day. It is generally eaten in two or three courses, first with spiced lentils and lastly with cool yogurt. Lemon rice is a wonderful variation. I tend to keep lemon rice very lightly spiced although some versions are quite fiery. For me, rice should be fairly neutral so that it can be enjoyed with a stronger-flavoured curry, but if you are eating this on its own, do feel free to spice it up to your taste with a few dried red chillies added with the cashew nuts. Serves 4

Preparation time: 10 minutes **Cooking time:** 25 minutes

300g (10oz) basmati rice, washed and drained
2 tablespoons sunflower oil
1 teaspoon mustard seeds
6 fresh curry leaves
10 cashew nuts
1 teaspoon turmeric powder
3 tablespoons lemon juice
Salt

1 Put the rice and double the quantity of water in a heavy-bottomed saucepan. Bring to the boil. Reduce the heat and simmer partially covered until done. Run a fork through to loosen the grains, cover the pan with a lid and reserve.

2 In a separate pan, heat the oil and fry the mustard seeds until they pop. Add the curry leaves and the cashew nuts. When the cashews are slightly brown, add the turmeric.

3 Remove from heat at once and pour in the lemon juice. Season with salt. Gently mix the rice into this mixture and serve immediately.

Komdicha Pulao

I often make this easy one-pot dish when I have unexpected guests or a couple of my girlfriends over. It only needs a raita such as the Potato and Yogurt Salad (page 123) to complete the meal. I always use chicken breast because I don't like the idea of bits of bones breaking into the rice when I mix the two together. You could use red onion for this recipe if you prefer the flavour. Serves 4

Preparation time: 10 minutes   **Cooking time:** 35 minutes

300g (10oz) basmati rice, washed and drained
2 tablespoons sunflower oil
1 large onion, finely sliced
2 teaspoons ginger-garlic paste
1 teaspoon turmeric powder
1 teaspoon chilli powder
300g (10oz) chicken breast, cut into 2.5cm (1in) cubes
2 tablespoons lemon juice
Salt

1 Put the rice and double the quantity of water in a heavy-bottomed saucepan. Bring to the boil. Reduce the heat and simmer partially covered until done. Run a fork through to loosen the grains, cover the pan with a lid and reserve.

2 Meanwhile, heat the oil in a wok. Fry the onion. When translucent, remove half of them and reserve. Continue to fry the remaining onion until dark golden in colour. Drain and reserve separately.

3 Put the translucent onion back into the wok and add the ginger-garlic paste. Fry for a few seconds.

4 Sprinkle in the spice powders and add the chicken. Stir to seal, until the chicken looks white instead of pink.

5 Add about 4 tablespoons hot water, cover the wok and cook until the chicken is tender and cooked through.

6 Remove from the heat, add the lemon juice and season with salt.

7 Gently stir in the cooked rice.

8 Sprinkle the golden fried onions on top and serve hot.

BROWN RICE WITH ONION AND PINENUTS

Pyazwala Pulao

The combination of rice and fried onions is very popular in Indian dishes. The onions add a sweet crispness to the bland rice. I have also added pinenuts for extra flavour. Serve this with Creamy Chicken Curry (page 82). A fresh green salad will also give the meal a lift. *Serves 4*

Preparation time: 10 minutes   **Cooking time:** 35 minutes

2 tablespoons sunflower oil
1 teaspoon cumin seeds
1 large onion, finely sliced
300g (10oz) basmati rice, washed and drained
Salt
2 tablespoons pinenuts
3 tablespoons coriander leaves, finely chopped

1 Heat the oil in a heavy-bottomed saucepan. Add the cumin seeds and stir for a few seconds until they darken.

2 Add the onion and keep stirring until it turns dark golden.

3 Add the rice and mix well. It should take on a caramel-like colour from the fried onions.

4 Season with salt and pour in 600ml (1¼ pints) hot water. Bring to the boil, reduce the heat and cook, partially covered until the rice is done. Cover the pan with a lid and reserve.

5 Meanwhile, dry roast the pinenuts in a small frying pan until they start to turn golden in colour. Run a fork through the rice to separate the grains and serve hot sprinkled with the pinenuts and coriander.

TOMATO RICE WITH MUSTARD

Sasuve Bhath

This south Indian recipe is a quick festive dish to make for easy entertaining on Sundays. I serve it with a nice vegetable dish such as Peas in Saffron-flavoured Yogurt (page 98) and a rich meat dish such as the Lamb with Fresh Figs (page 61). It also tastes delicious eaten with natural yogurt and a spicy relish. I try to use very concentrated tomato purée for the best colour and most intense flavour. *Serves 4*

Preparation time: 10 minutes   **Cooking time:** 35 minutes

2 tablespoons sunflower oil
1 teaspoon black mustard seeds
1 teaspoon cumin seeds
1 teaspoon mild chilli powder
2 tablespoons concentrated tomato purée
Salt
300g (10oz) basmati rice, washed and drained
2 tablespoons coriander leaves, chopped

1 Heat the oil in a heavy-bottomed pan and fry the mustard seeds until they begin to pop. Add the cumin seeds and stir a couple of times.

2 Reduce the heat, sprinkle in the chilli powder then add the tomato purée. Increase the heat and add 4 tablespoons water. Bring to a bubble.

3 Season with salt and add the rice. Pour in 600ml (1¼ pints) hot water. Bring to the boil and reduce the heat. Simmer, partially covered, until the rice is done. Remove from the heat and run a fork through the rice to loosen the grains and cover the pan with a lid and steam for 3–4 minutes.

5 Serve hot, drizzled with lemon juice and sprinkled with coriander.

Hara Pulao

Green curry paste is made with herbs and therefore has a fresh summery taste at any time of the year. The basic paste can be used with a variety of ingredients such as prawns, chicken (my favourite), cauliflower and potatoes. Be sure to use very fresh mint and discard any brown or wilted leaves as this herb is at the heart of this delicious rice dish. Serves 4

Preparation time: 20 minutes   **Cooking time:** 35 minutes

for the green curry paste
1 bunch fresh coriander, washed and drained
1 bunch fresh mint, washed and drained
2 teaspoons ginger-garlic paste
2 fresh green chillies, roughly chopped
Salt

Sunflower oil for deep frying

4 slices white bread, crusts removed, cut into 1cm (1/2in) cubes
300g (10oz) basmati rice, washed and drained
2 tablespoons lemon juice

1 Tear the coriander and the mint into the bowl of a blender. Add the ginger-garlic paste and the green chillies. Whizz to as fine a paste as possible adding a little water at a time to hasten the process. The final paste should be the consistency of thick custard.

2 Season with salt and set aside.

3 Put the rice in a heavy-bottomed pan and add 300ml (10fl oz) hot water. Stir in the green herby paste.

4 Bring to the boil, reduce the heat, partially cover the pan and simmer until the rice is done. You may need to add a little water if the rice is still raw at the centre. Remove from the heat and run a fork through the rice to loosen the grains. Cover the pan with a lid and reserve.

5 Meanwhile, heat the oil in a deep saucepan or wok. Fry the cubes of bread until golden brown in colour, remove with a slotted spoon and drain on kitchen paper.

6 Serve the rice hot, garnished with the crisp croûtons.

Index